D1020103

THE RESPONSIBILITY VIRUS

The Responsibility Virus

How Control Freaks,
Shrinking Violets—and the
Rest of Us—Can Harness
the Power of True Partnership

ROGER L. MARTIN

BASIC
BOOKS

A Member of the Perseus Books Group

Copyright © 2002 by Roger L. Martin

Published by Basic Books,
A Member of the Perseus Books Group

All rights reserved. Printed in the United States of America. No part of this book may be reproduced in any manner whatsoever without written permission except in the case of brief quotations embodied in critical articles and reviews. For information, address Basic Books, 387 Park Avenue South, New York, NY 10016–8810.

Designed by *Trish Wilkinson*

Library of Congress Cataloging-in-Publication Data
Martin, Roger L.
    The responsibility virus : how control freaks, shrinking violets—and the rest of us—can harness the power of true partnership / Roger L. Martin.
    Includes index.
    ISBN 0–465–04410–7
    1. Leadership. 2. Management. 3. Responsibility. 4. Organizational effectiveness. 5. Interpersonal relations. I. Title.
HD57.7 .M3925 2002
658.4'092—dc21   2002007244

02 03 04 05 / 10 9 8 7 6 5 4 3 2 1

Contents

PART FOUR

Fighting the Responsibility Virus

CONCLUSION

Preface

Why do so many leaders fail despite their hardest effort? Why do so many executives act as aggressive leaders one minute and passive followers the next? Why, when managers attempt to collaborate, does 1 + 1 typically equal less than 2? Why do large organizations often fail to harvest the "advantages of scale" they're supposed to have over smaller organizations?

These questions baffled me during the first dozen years of my consulting career. Working with senior executives on issues of strategy for twenty years, I was in a privileged position. From close range I was able to watch chairmen, CEOs, and boards of directors, as well as discuss with them their reasoning for decisions and explore their feelings about themselves, their organizations, and their colleagues. Sometimes, with their permission, I tape-recorded their thoughts. At other times, I asked them to write down personal cases describing how they made decisions. And sometimes I just listened, watched, and took notes.

Over those twenty years, I have worked for a truly wide range of clients. Many were very large global firms, including Alcan, AT&T, Barrick, CAE, Herman Miller, Hiram Walker, Honeywell, Inco, Koch Industries, Moore Corporation, Pacific Gas and Electric, Procter and Gamble, Servicemaster, and Thomson Corporation. Many others were medium-sized national firms, disproportionately in two areas: the media sector, including broadcasters, magazines, newspapers, and advertising agencies; and professional service firms, including law firms, consulting firms, and brokerage houses. My clients also came from the public sector, where I worked for both county governments and large global nongovernment organizations.

The cases you'll find illustrating *The Responsibility Virus* are drawn from my work at the senior levels with a selection of these clients. The cases describe real people facing, struggling with, and often succumbing to real challenges. Because the events described are often extremely painful and embarrassing for those involved, I have disguised the cases (except the one involving me in Chapter 9). The alterations of specific industries, locations, names, and titles will obscure them to anybody not involved but will not confuse or water down the business lessons to be learned. Those portrayed here will likely recognize themselves and their organizations, and in this respect I apologize in advance to the extent that the reading may bring back unpleasant memories.

I wrote this book in order to help people avoid the natural predisposition to mishandle responsibility in ways that undermine their goals and their well-being. After working for so long with the best and brightest, I have come to believe that everyone is highly susceptible to what I describe as the Responsibility Virus. The Virus sets up leaders and followers for failure and for developing less quickly than they could or should. And because neither sees the Virus, both are doomed to repeat their errors.

Fortunately, we can be inoculated against the Responsibility Virus in ways that are practical and doable. The diagnosis was clear by 1993, the prescriptions only by about 1999. It was time for me to write the book only after I had paired the two. My text is approximately one-third diagnosis and two-thirds prescription. My intent in the last two-thirds is to create a set of simple, actionable tools that anyone in any organization can use to inoculate themselves against the Responsibility Virus and become a more effective leader or follower.

I have many people to thank for this book. First and foremost are my clients. By seeking my help on their strategy problems, they also provided me with a window on a dynamic that forms the foundation of this book. A number of them became important thinking partners on the themes of the book, including Wolfgang Berndt, Tina Brown, Rob Harvey, Patricia Meredith, and Jean-Francois Rischard—my most sincere thanks and appreciation to each one of them.

A trio of academic mentors provided me with a lens powerful enough to capture the data and process the signals; chief among those individuals is Chris Argyris, Professor Emeritus at Harvard Business School, who has helped me since 1987, and whose research and thinking have been instrumental. But I would never have worked with those clients on important strategy issues had it not been for a second academic mentor, Michael Porter, Bishop William Lawrence University Professor at Harvard University, with whom I have worked on strategy for almost twenty years. Since 1995, Michael Jensen, Professor Emeritus at Harvard Business School, has helped shape my thinking and provided great encouragement to me.

To get the idea from my head to manuscript to book required enormous support, which started with Malcolm Gladwell, who introduced me to literary agent Tina Bennett, of Janklow and Nesbitt. One could not wish for a better agent, friend, and supporter than Tina. Not only are her intellectual fingerprints on the book, her drive and determination to see the project through to a happy conclusion provided the wind in the sails during the occasional bleak period. Tina, in turn, introduced me to my beloved editor at Basic Books, Liz Maguire, who believed in the project from the beginning and steered it with consummate skill through four years and two publishing houses of development. It is a much better book because of Liz's advice and counsel. With Liz there was never a shove when a nudge would do.

One of the cleverest things she did was introduce me to consummate wordsmith William Patrick. Thankfully for me, Bill was willing to come to the aid of an author long on ideas and short on writing experience. Thanks to Bill's rearranging, reshaping, shortening, and smoothing, the story shines through much more brightly than before his pen touched the manuscript. My Rotman School colleague, Professor Mihnea Moldoveanu, provided invaluable assistance in both improving the intellectual rigor of the manuscript and setting it within the context of the broader academic literature, much of which he introduced to me.

Along the way, many others provided invaluable help. Diana Smith of the firm Action Design worked side by side with me for several years and introduced me to the concept of the Frame Experiment (see Chapter 8), as well as coined the term "dueling ladders" (see Figure 7.2). Consulting colleague Sandra Pocharski, who throughout my career helped convert my ideas to compelling visual images, drew the first version of the Choice Structuring Process (Figure 7.3). My younger brother Terry Martin read the manuscript several times and gave helpful advice. My longtime colleague Kathy Halliday provided editorial and production help from the time that the words "Responsibility Virus" first escaped my lips, and she was recently joined in that effort by Suzanne Spragge, who became part of my staff two years ago.

My wife, Nancy, and my three children, Lloyd, Jennifer, and Daniel, were good and supportive sports as I holed up in our cottage bedroom writing and rewriting rather than playing, perhaps as I should have been, in the sun. Without their support the Responsibility Virus would still exist, but this book wouldn't.

Finally, I thank my parents. This book attempts to integrate the business insights I learned from my father, Lloyd Martin, with the behavioral insights I learned from my mother, Delphine Martin.

This book has been written from the heart to influence the hearts and minds of the readers. I hope it resonates with you and provides you with a few ideas that will help make your life more productive.

Do We Need
Another Hero?

Mayor Rudolph Giuliani became a national hero by virtue of his leadership during the 9/11 crisis in New York in 2001. Immediately following the attacks on the World Trade Center, Giuliani was all over New York, night and day, at the WTC site, at firehouses and hospitals and morgues, and in the financial district, overseeing the rescue and recovery and reassuring the public, while also helping to get the New York Stock Exchange, the heartbeat of the world's financial markets, up and running again within a week.

And yet the mayor's finest hour, which led to his selection as *Time* magazine's 2001 "Person of the Year," as well as an honorary knighthood from the British crown, came in just the last few weeks of a long administration during which his autocratic style took considerable heat and during which his

results were often mixed. In dealing with the New York public schools, for instance, Giuliani failed miserably.

What made the difference? Why was his leadership so effective in the one instance, and so ineffective in the other?

Fundamentally, the difference emerges from the initial
message that this leader sent.

To all observers, the World Trade Center was a crisis beyond the capacity of any one person, or any one group, to rec-
tify. Appropriately, Mayor Giuliani's message to the city and
to the world was, "We're all in this together." He signaled that
he would give all that he had, but he left no doubt that he
would need the talent and energy of thousands of other,
equally dedicated individuals in order to succeed. As the city
dug out from the rubble, he carried through like the mud-
splattered colonel in a World War II movie, leading the charge,
inspiring the troops, mucking through the trenches alongside
the workers as they carried out the wounded, then laid the ca-
bles that would once again light up the Big Board.

With the New York public schools, the mayor's message
was quite different. To the educational administration and
staff, in essence he said, "I'm in charge and you're not."
Faced with a crisis, he tried to seize control, but far from
inviting collaboration, he made it clear that the first rule of
his leadership was, "My way or the highway." As a result,
the hundreds of people down the line who needed to throw
their collective shoulders to the wheel in order to achieve
success retreated to the margins. Reduced to the role of passive followers, they sat back and watched him fail—and in
the end probably enjoyed it.

Take-charge leadership is the stuff of Hollywood and history books, deeply ingrained in our consciousness. In times
of crisis, what often surfaces is our reverence for the "man
on the horse" who will grip the reins firmly and make us feel

safe. And yet, in most cases such heroic leadership, misapplied, not only fails to inspire and engage, it produces passivity and alienation instead.

The George Washingtons and Winston Churchills, the truly heroic leaders who inspire commitment from their followers in time of overwhelming danger, are cherished in large part because they are so rare. The single-handed feats of derring-do of a Clint Eastwood or a Bruce Willis take place on film because they are, by and large, far removed from reality.

John Kennedy's Peace Corps is still going strong forty years on, and Newt Gingrich's Contract With America was forgotten after a single term, in part because of the differing leadership styles inherent in each man. Gingrich brilliantly took issues from the grass-roots level, made them national, and won a Republican congressional majority. However, his message with the Contract With America was: "Vote for us, then sit back and watch us perform. We'll take care of it for you." By contrast, the Peace Corps was the embodiment of Kennedy's most memorable line: "Ask not what your country can do for you; ask what you can do for your country."

When leaders assume "heroic" responsibility for making the critical choices facing their organizations, when their reaction to problems is to go it alone, work harder, do more, to be more heroic still, with no collaboration and sharing of the leadership burden, their "heroism" is often their undoing.

Would-be heroic leaders get plenty of assistance in creating failure from well-intentioned subordinates, who believe that when the chips are down, leaders should be given the latitude to jump into the fray and take control, whether their leaderly capabilities are up to the task or not. At the slightest flinch from subordinates, leaders are expected to unilaterally assert control and cover for them by taking a wildly disproportionate share of the responsibility while subordinates stand back and watch.

Humans have a natural tendency toward all-or-nothing thinking when it comes to leadership and responsibility, and our responses are dynamic and infectious.

One person makes a quick assessment of the situation and tries to take charge. But the strong statement "I'm in charge . . ." almost always carries with it the unspoken ". . . and you're not." In most cases, as with the New York public schools, the signal "I'm in charge and you're not" prompts the other party to send a corresponding signal: "Fine. I understand. You're in charge and I'm not." Those initial signals, both the heroic and the passive, begin a cascade of reactions that lead to eventual failure.

The heroic party reacts to the first flinch of hesitation, the first sign of passivity, by trying to fill what he sees as a void. This causes the passive party to see himself as being further marginalized, which prompts a further retreat, until he has abdicated all responsibility. And so it goes.

Near the end of the cycle the passive party is distant, cynical, and lethargic. Then the heroic party, contemptuous of the other and angry for having to bear the full weight alone, collapses under the burden.

But it's not only the heroic leader who gets crushed. The taint of failure is distributed to everyone involved. This leadership model undermines collaboration, generates mistrust and misunderstanding, and eventually causes the choice-making skills of both leaders and followers to decline.

The dynamic of heroic leadership, unilaterally imposed, can infect any relationship, and it can spread through an organization like a virus. It's also true that the roles are not fixed. The same person can be the would-be hero in one situation and the passive follower in the next. But what I call the "Responsibility Virus" always begins with the germ of fear.

In numerous studies, psychologists have shown just how much we dread having done the wrong thing, so much so that we go to great lengths to avoid making choices, or even viewing ourselves as choosers. Irving Janis, a social psychologist and leading scholar of group behavior, and his co-workers found that the heart rate of participants in their experiments quickened considerably as they were about to find out whether or not they had made the "right choice," the one that would align with their preferences.[1] And the social and cognitive psychologist Leon Festinger showed that many people avoid choices between options that are at least at first blush equally desirable by postponing them, or by pretending there is no choice to be made because the options are identical, or by pretending that the choice has already been made for them, or by distorting the negative aspects of one option and the positive aspects of another to the point that, once again, there is no choice at all to be made.[2]

The presence of colleagues with whom we could share the burden of choice-making responsibility should have the effect of getting us beyond worries about regret and failure, and thus enhancing our ability to choose well. Sadly, the opposite happens time and time again. In situations in which responsibility could be reasonably and effectively shared, the fear of failure tends to trigger one of the two extreme responses we've just described. Both undermine the possibility of productive collaboration.

The Responsibility Virus is as pervasive—and as ancient— as the common cold. The philosopher Hegel described the tendency to flip from dominance to subservience, what he called "the master-slave dialect," as being one of the driving forces of human history.[3]

It appears in contexts both trivial and tragic. You can see it on the basketball court when a gifted player is too dominant. A solo performance by someone of exceptional talent can get the job done for a while, but then the rest of the teammates become disengaged. Being shut out of the offense leads to standing around on defense, which leads to a losing season, no matter how great the shooting statistics racked up by their MVP.

In its most insidious manifestations, the Responsibility Virus has played a role in many a business scandal, and worse, many a political atrocity. Whenever parties within any organizational structure claim victim status, when they say they were "duped" or were "just following orders," we know there's been an outbreak of the Virus.

No better example could be found than the Enron debacle. With almost $100 billion of shareholder value wiped out, thousands of jobs lost, and retirements marred, party after party has come forward and, in what appears to be a genuinely proffered view, said: "It wasn't my fault. I was just doing my job." How could this be? How could accountants, lawyers, investment bankers, senior management, internal auditors, politicians, and regulators all be faultless in the face of a debacle of epic proportions? The answer is the narrow perfectionism brought on by the Responsibility Virus. Spurred by the fear of failure, each player defined his job sufficiently narrowly that he could claim success to himself and others even as the gaps between each narrow world brought a giant firm to its knees.

While the Virus is pervasive, it's only recently been identified. That's why attempts to remedy the problem heretofore have been off the mark. In most cases, the attempted remedy has been to alter organizational structure as if formal lines of authority and job descriptions were the only features that mattered.

The most dominant voice in this chorus has been the "empowerment" school, which argues that responsibility is held too centrally at the top. The theory is that a military-style, hierarchical command-and-control approach disempowers members of the organization who, feeling like pawns in a game or puppets controlled by a powerful master, underachieve relative to their actual abilities. This line of thinking suggests that if leaders loosened their controlling grip and relentlessly pushed down choice-making responsibility and accountability in their organizations, they would unleash a tidal wave of enthusiastic action and collaboration by their now-empowered colleagues. According to this argument, such empowered organizations would out-compete their command-and-control competitors.

I watched this movement play out in a number of my consulting clients and saw little of its promise realized. Instead, I witnessed a high rate of failure. "Empowered" employees rarely felt the enthusiasm predicted and did not produce the tidal wave of positive action forecast. Throwing high levels of responsibility on them on the basis of the empowerment doctrine rather than in relation to their underlying capabilities was more likely to produce disempowerment, confusion, and low morale.

My many years of strategy consulting to myriad diverse organizations convinced me that the roots of the Responsibility Virus are not to be found on an org chart but within our deepest human motivations. Like the gamblers studied by Ellen Langer, who want to take responsibility for their predictions once they win, but blame chance whenever their hunches turn out to be wrong, it is human nature to claim credit when things go well and to avoid blame when they go badly.[4] It's a matter of minimizing the risks of social failure while maximizing the personal gains of positive events. These are the inner drives that push us to the extremes of over-responsibility and under-responsibility.

The choice is often triggered by our reaction to other actions taken by the other parties involved, even if the reaction is minor. A small flinch or look of confusion can provoke a "heroic" response. A confident expression or firm tone can provoke a passive response. In turn, the other parties involved make decisions based on the actions they see taken, decisions to become more over- or under-responsible.

But the infection doesn't stop there. The Virus propels the heroic leader to a failure generated by taking on more responsibility than any one person can carry. But then, as over-responsible leaders approach the point of failure, they do an abrupt turnaround, flipping to an under-responsible stance in order to insulate themselves from the pain and responsibility they see looming. "I was set up," leaders often say. "Nobody else did their part." "It was never meant to be." But by suddenly denying responsibility, the leader sends a message to the passive followers.

Although they sat back and watched, putting the responsibility for success in the hands of the heroic leader, the followers are not insulated from the outcome. They experience two things simultaneously: first, the pain of failure; second, the experience of the heroic leader's sudden reversal. This doubly traumatic experience jolts these followers into their own extreme reaction—flipping to over-responsibility, making sure that they are never again put into a position of being dependent on a leader who lets them down.

This vacillation between over- and under-responsibility is an endless loop. Fear of failure drives them into an initial extreme position. The extreme positions of over- and under-responsibility drive them into failure. Failure causes them to flip into the other extreme. And so on.

Advising leaders to stop being heroic and exhorting passive followers to become more aggressive doesn't get the job done. Heroic leaders and passive followers are pursuing what they feel, at that time and place, to be the optimal course of action. And organizational fixes don't help, because distributing or centralizing power doesn't change the personal dynamic in this intensely personal exchange. Unless you attack this dynamic of fear itself, heroic leaders and passive followers will pop up where they are not supposed to be, no matter what the formal organizational structure.

Merely adding players to a choice-making situation doesn't help either, as the literature on "groupthink" makes clear,[5] as does the literature on conformity to group norms and actions.[6] In those cases, the presence of others in a choice-making situation simply makes the decisionmaker less sure of his or her own authority to render a judgment.

This state of affairs creates no end of frustration and an almost-inexhaustible supply of material for Dilbert cartoons. Groups formed to make decisions or better decisions flounder and fail. Frustration with decisions by committee leads to a clarion call for "single-point accountability."

The net result of these all-too-human dynamics is that, as firms get larger and can dedicate more and more managers to a given problem, they don't get better choices; if anything, they get significantly worse ones.

While the choices get bigger and more complex, the resources that can be applied effectively to choices become no greater, because collaboration is ineffective or absent, neutralized by the Responsibility Virus. Thus decisionmaking failures become more prevalent and the call is for leadership that is yet more heroic. The expectation of yet more heroic leadership merely intensifies the viral strain, which causes still more failure, followed by a call for yet more heroic leadership, and so on and so on.

It is no wonder then that there is such a fascination with heroic leaders and, in the business world, the cult of the CEO. But this merely feeds the Virus, creating ever-greater levels of mistrust and misunderstanding. Heroic leaders, who don't understand how their own actions help create passive followers, grow to see the followers as pathetic and undeserving of their leadership. Passive followers, who similarly are blind to their role in creating isolated, heroic leaders, grow to see the leaders as domineering and unsympathetic. Each questions the motives of the other and resentment takes over.

As failure looms, followers become angry with leaders for letting them down. Leaders become angry with followers for not lifting a finger to help. Neither is able to see his or her role in creating the pathology and the failure, and instead blames the other. Both resolve never to let this happen again. But to ensure that it won't, they simultaneously flip to opposite extremes of responsibility, which makes it likely that it indeed will happen again, because nothing has been learned from the failure.

The combination of failure with the failure to learn from failure produces little advancement in the decisionmaking skills of leaders. Rather than learning from the failed choices, the passive followers simply blame the leader, which means that they don't test and improve their choice-making skills either.

These skills can atrophy just as surely as my tennis game would atrophy if I spent all my time up against players much weaker or much stronger than I am. Erosion in these skills is hugely threatening in a world of large, complex networked organizations and coalitions and alliances in which joint choice-making and effective collaboration is a necessity. Without better skills in productively sharing responsibility, these twenty-first-century organizations and organizational forms will lead to chaos and inertia.

During two decades of work with organizations struggling to overcome the Responsibility Virus, I have devised a set of tools that get beyond the organizational chart and go to the heart of the problem.

The first tool is "The Choice Structuring Process," a method that helps group members collaborate productively with one another rather than leaping instinctively to heroic leadership or passive followership. It harnesses the power of a group to make more inspired and robust decisions, and commit to them, than any individual could achieve alone.

The second tool—"The Frame Experiment"—helps individuals who are stuck in over- or under-responsibility and experiencing mistrust or misunderstanding to improve their relationship and their ability to collaborate with the individual in question.

The third—"The Responsibility Ladder"—is a developmental tool that helps subordinates work with their bosses to build their ability to take on responsibility and prevent their bosses from becoming over-responsible.

The fourth tool is a more productive "Redefinition of Leadership and Followership" that helps both leaders and followers avoid falling into the extremes of over- and under-responsibility.

Taken together, these tools can help each of us fight to suppress the heroic leader who lurks below the surface in every tough decisionmaking situation. They can help us deal with our fear of failure in a way that allows a different model of leading and following to emerge. The payoff is better collaboration, better decisions for our organizations, better understanding and trust of our colleagues, and faster skill-building for all of us.

PART 1

Dynamics of the Responsibility Virus

CHAPTER 1

Understanding the Responsibility Virus

Michael is the publisher of *Wapshot*, a leading national magazine. Young, lean, and aggressive, he's the kind of executive who burns off extra energy at the gym five times a week.

With a track record for turnarounds, Michael has had a meteoric career. Still, *Wapshot* is a big job for him, his biggest jump yet. Long considered a rising star, he received extensive press attention with this appointment, and he knows that everyone is still watching. A success here would consolidate his position as one of the leading figures in magazine publishing. Any failure would be a very public humiliation.

And the task at *Wapshot* is no pushover. Before Michael's arrival, advertising revenue, the lifeblood of the modern magazine, had been in slow decline. His initial analysis of the situation yielded two straightforward objectives. First, he had to turn around the decline in number of ad pages per issue. Second, he had to increase the average price charged for each page. This was the only way to stabilize the magazine's revenue base and shore up its financial condition.

Nobody ever doubted Michael's ability to "bring in the pages." That was the word on him from his previous publishing jobs. He was famous, if not infamous, for pushing salespeople, challenging them to keep up with his own frenetic pace. Nobody ever relished going into Michael's office with bad news on sales volume.

But progress on revenue increase is behind plan, and this is bad news that will spawn further bad news. Advertising page totals for each leading magazine are collected and published twice yearly in an industry bible. If the results for any publication don't look good, that book gets a negative buzz, and the sales force has a harder time convincing advertisers that their magazine is a "must buy." Michael knows that *Wapshot*'s owner, Louis, pays close attention to the buzz and is not afraid to try to offset bad buzz with positive buzz by announcing the installation of yet another rising star as its new publisher.

That's why a phone call earlier in the day had Michael apoplectic. He had hired his VP of sales, Caroline, as one of his first moves as publisher. Attractive and always impeccably dressed, she was known as a sales whiz with enough personality and charm to get anyone to do almost anything. But she had struggled since coming to *Wapshot*. This was a more complex sell than her previous challenges. Advertisers had more choices and didn't absolutely need this magazine to fill out their media buy.

The telephone call was a heads up to Michael that a big computer firm was threatening to drop *Wapshot* from its ad plan. Caroline wanted to come over and talk to Michael before meeting with the firm and its agency to try to save those pages.

When Caroline comes into Michael's office, her charm and pizzazz are nowhere in sight. Head down, shoulders slumped, she looks as if she'd just wandered in off the street. "This is a really big meeting," she mutters, as if to herself. "Maybe you should come along, Michael. Maybe you should even help me make the pitch."

Michael, still reeling from the bad news about the account, is shaken even more by Caroline's obviously shattered confidence. "Sure, I'll come along," he says. But as he looks again at her hangdog expression, those vacant eyes, he says, "If I do, though, maybe I should take the lead. It'd look weird to have the publisher at the meeting just sitting at the back of the room." He forces a smile, and then tells her, "You work up a presentation . . . then we can talk about it."

Caroline takes a crack at writing the pitch, but when Michael looks at the first draft his anxiety skyrockets. He takes the presentation and rewrites the whole thing, all the while wondering why Caroline isn't capable of better work. In the end, Michael not only attends the meeting, he makes the pitch, wowing everyone with speaking skills honed through long experience. He leads the follow-up discussion, too, leaving Caroline sitting like a chump on the sidelines.

Caroline appreciates the help, but, as she watches her boss in action, her self-confidence shrinks even more. In the days and weeks that follow, with Michael's masterly presentation still looming over her, she recedes further into the background on the computer account. And because Michael made the pitch, he is now implicated in servicing the account. He has to be directly involved in order to complete the "rescue" plan.

Over time, as other key pitches need to be prepared, Caroline again comes to Michael for advice. Seeing how tentative she's become, Michael offers not just to advise but also to help. Preparation for and execution of other pitches start to eat up more and more of his time. The presentations are fabulous, but all this extra work is cutting into his ability to manage other functions, not the least of which is the long-term strategic thinking he should be doing as publisher.

Michael begins to bemoan Caroline's lack of initiative. "She acts like a sheep," he tells himself. "She waits till things are bad. Then she comes for help and I have to step in and save the day. It's getting me down. I never seem to be able to get around to the rest of my job. I keep getting dragged down into the minutiae of advertising sales, with no end in sight."

Caroline senses Michael's frustration, and his obvious lack of confidence in her undermines her own shaky sense of self. More and more she defers to Michael in meetings. Increasingly, she equivocates on decisions that she is fully competent to make.

Meanwhile, Michael is working to the point of exhaustion, feeling the weight of the world on his shoulders, and getting nowhere. With every passing day his employees seem increasingly paralytic, yet for him every day feels like a fire drill. And worst of all, he feels painfully alone. He can barely tolerate talking to the rest of the sheep on his staff who are making his life miserable.

As Caroline watches Michael race around from meeting to meeting and pitch to pitch, his actions appear to her now as disorganized, desperate, and not very leader-like. She finds his increasingly curt and sarcastic demeanor toward her demotivating. His tendency to go directly to her salespeople without involving her makes her lose face, while it intimidates her salespeople, who complain about Michael's aggressive manner. She finds herself questioning her role, questioning her capabilities, and wondering if she's cut out for the job.

Despite all Michael's feverish effort, advertising sales trend further south. In a tearful outburst Caroline offers her resignation, citing her frustration with the position Michael has put her in and her inability to work with him. Michael is flabbergasted. He talks her back from the edge, but he can't believe her ingratitude for all of his efforts.

Looking at the same downturn from his perspective as owner, Louis turns up the heat on everyone. Michael responds by working even harder, but no amount of effort allows him to rise above the daily scramble. Unbeknownst to Michael, Louis begins making a few calls, trying to get a lead on the next rising star in the magazine business, just in case.

The offices of *Wapshot* are infected with the Responsibility Virus, an opportunistic virus, triggered by the experience of failure.

In this case, the computer firm's decision to remove the magazine from its ad plan was a huge, symbolic blow that undermined both Michael's and Caroline's immunity. Michael knew that his first priority was to improve the magazine's performance on advertising sales. But the upswing never happened, and the loss of this important computer account was very much a step in the wrong direction.

Hiring Caroline had been one of Michael's most important and visible managerial decisions thus far, and now it looked like a bad one. For her part, Caroline felt a personal sense of failure over the loss of an account that was clearly hers to protect. She had been struggling to meet her targets even before the computer firm began to pull away. Both Michael and Caroline were rattled and embarrassed. In terms of the Responsibility Virus, the atmosphere of fear and failure had left these two immunosuppressed.

How could it have been different? How could they have responded to ward off the infection and avoid a full-blown outbreak of the disease?

Instead of leaping into the fray, Michael could have checked his own fears and provided encouragement, assuring Caroline that losing accounts happens despite solid efforts (which is entirely true), and that it can be overcome. He could have offered her ideas on how to plot a campaign to get back the account and how to structure the new presentation. He could have coached Caroline on what to do at the meeting. He could have supported her as she led the meeting with the computer firm and its agency. All of these steps would have had the effect of helping Caroline improve her skills, make higher-quality choices, and step up to higher responsibility.

For her part, Caroline could have been less quick to abdicate. She could have signaled her desire to improve without signaling helplessness and despair. She could have asked for Michael's help in reviewing the choices she had made on the account to understand what he might have done differently. She could have asked to brainstorm with him on the content of the new pitch. These steps would have kept her in the game at a level of responsibility consistent with her capabilities, neither above nor below.

These steps would have constituted productive collaboration—the utilization of both of their skill-sets in combination to produce an outcome superior to the outcome of either working alone. Instead, Michael assumed responsibility for engineering success, and Caroline relinquished it.

Had either Michael or Caroline been asked about their intentions going into the meeting, neither would have stated this outcome as a goal. Yet it happened. Why? Because the rush to an extreme in the assumption or abdication of responsibility is a deeply ingrained aspect of human nature.

Many of our basic emotional responses have an all-or-nothing property that can be traced all the way down to the level of muscle contractions. Each muscle fiber can either "fire" or "not fire." This dichotomy is especially true when fear is involved. Fear engages our fight-or-flight response, a set of instantaneous physiological changes, such as blood rushing to the skin, which developed deep in our evolutionary history as an emergency alert system to get us out of trouble. Back then, only two responses to danger made sense: fight, or run away. All, or nothing.

Which response we choose—fight or flight, seize responsibility or flee from it—is mutual, tacit, and largely unconscious. We signal our choice like two joggers approaching one another on a narrow path. The instant one veers ever so slightly in one direction, the other takes the cue and begins diverting to the opposite side. They pass each other without words, without bumping, and without really knowing what caused each to move.

The Responsibility Virus moves from one party to the other without acknowledgment, as if caused by invisible microbes.

Responding in fight mode, Michael seizes a high level of responsibility, which sends a clear message to Caroline to take on a correspondingly lower level of responsibility, the flight mode. Cornered by the fear of failure, he chooses the rescue strategy, the nature of the presentation, and the

FIGURE 1.1   Characteristic Response to Threat or Experience
of Failure

form of interaction with the client at the presentation. Psychologically in flight from the same fear of failure, Caroline tacitly—perhaps even unconsciously—accepts.

We also could argue the alternative interpretation—that Caroline initiates the Virus by first signaling her abdication of responsibility. She explicitly invites Michael to come along and help make the pitch, but her lack of confidence implicitly invites him to take over all the key choices. He receives the signal and acts accordingly.

Regardless of who starts and how, at the slightest hint of a move by one, the other takes the opposite tack. Flooding us with stress hormones, the fight-or-flight response allows no time for considered judgments. It demands immediate, instinctive reactions that are all too often inappropriate amid the complexities of the modern world.

When we assume leadership and full responsibility in the wake of failure, we might see ourselves as heroic and self-sacrificing. We may see the other party as a sheep who would be lost without our leadership. We might begin to assume that they would be incapable of accepting and fulfilling new responsibility. As a consequence, we all too often move preemptively to seize further responsibility. At the same time, as our burden grows we start harboring resentment toward our fearful colleague for their dependence. Increasingly, we see ourselves as the only reliable party, who therefore *must* take on a disproportionate share of responsibility despite the personal burden and sacrifice that may entail.

Powered by frustration and anger, both at Caroline and at the impossible position he finds himself in, Michael can see no option but to go further down the path of over-responsibility. Feeling threatened from all sides, he develops a hair-trigger for seizing responsibility. Caroline's slightest hesitation prompts him to seize more.

Because Michael is far more experienced and skilled than Caroline, each individual responsibility he takes on is well within his capabilities. However, advertising sales is Caroline's job, not Michael's. Michael already has a job—publisher. And for Michael, the position as publisher is a significant step up in his own career development, stretching his capabilities well enough without adding day-to-day responsibility for advertising sales.

Eventually, the overall responsibility taken on exceeds even Michael's more developed capabilities and he begins to falter. In this he illustrates the typical path from a triggering event when it prompts us to assume singular responsibility for success, as shown in Figure 1.2.

As Caroline continues her flight from responsibility, taking on more and more the role of passive follower, she begins to see herself as uneasily dependent on a leader whom she views as essential but not fully reliable. She wants Michael to make pitches because he is more skilled, but she wishes he wouldn't be in such a rush, racing into meetings at the last moment, appearing distracted. All the same, Michael is great at selling, and Caroline sees herself as ever less capable by

FIGURE 1.2   The Eventual Consequence of
            Over-Responsibility

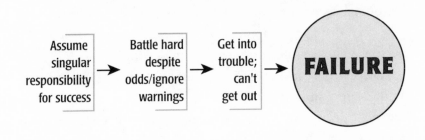

comparison. She continues to recede, becoming less engaged in her own job.

However, even as she abdicates responsibility, she holds Michael increasingly responsible for any subsequent failure. She begins to resent his "imperious" and "controlling" style. He seems to make all the choices, often without so much as consulting her. In client meetings, she feels that he cuts her off and acts dismissively toward her. This, in Caroline's view, makes it ever harder for her to gain the confidence of clients in the way Michael does. After the meetings, clients call Michael to follow up. They don't call Caroline.

For Caroline, her first instinctive step toward under-responsibility also sets in motion a sequence of steps that leads eventually—and inevitably—to painful failure.

The Responsibility Virus becomes an enclosed, self-reflexive world. It produces data that reinforces our view that we are correct, which reinforces the actions that produce still more reinforcing data.

Michael thinks Caroline is acting passively and Caroline thinks Michael is acting aggressively. Caroline responds by backing off, which convinces Michael that he is indeed correct

FIGURE 1.3   The Eventual Consequence of
             Under-Responsibility

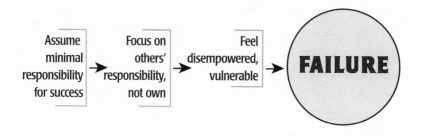

in his assessment of her passivity. He responds to this confirmation by being more aggressive still, which provides data to Caroline that she, too, was right all along. So regardless of whether they were right in the first instance, their snap judgments seem borne out by subsequent behavior.

Not only do we create self-fulfilling expectations of the other's capabilities, we also reinforce the negative views of one another's character and motives. The leader sees the follower as irresponsible, lazy, and uncommitted. The follower sees the leader as imperialistic, disrespectful, and belligerent. With these views in our heads, we become polarized and distant. We spend less time interacting. We stop trying to test whether our negative perceptions of the other are valid. In doing so, we reduce the possibility that we will ever communicate in ways that overcome the situation we have created.

Naive notions of causality reinforce this polarized, either/ or thinking. Psychologists such as Ellen Langer have demonstrated that control is something that most of us want more of,[1] but other studies, such as those by Thomas Gilovich, demonstrate our belief that responsibility cannot be partitioned.[2] In other words, if you're in control, then I can't be.

Enclosed, self-reflexive, all-or-nothing ways of thinking make for a negative prognosis. Instead of losing its virulence, the Virus actually gains strength as it passes back and forth, making it ever more difficult for the parties to overcome. Everyone feels a little queasy and knows something is wrong, and yet no one is quite sure what it is. In the absence of direct communications about the dynamic, each of us is left with our own unshakable, negative assessment of the other person, and a sickening feeling of foreboding.

The foreboding is well placed. As we've seen, the initial move to over-responsibility or under-responsibility usually ends in failure. Failure, or at least fear of failure, is of course where the whole sequence began. Unfortunately, the second failure simply spurs another cycle of the Virus, spinning in an endless loop until the whole dynamic crashes.

As the Virus plays out, the under-responsible party, at the point of failure, flips to over-responsibility, and the over-responsible party flips to under-responsibility.

The flip can result from frustration with the circumstances leading up to the failure, or it can occur in an attempt to protect ourselves from the pain of failure. When we are the over-responsible party we tend to say: "I did everything I could, worked myself to the bone, and had to struggle alone surrounded by ingrates. I've had enough. Somebody else had better step up to the plate. And for a change, I am going to sit back and watch."

When we are under-responsible, we tend to say: "I put myself in the hands of the leader who brushed me and my efforts aside. I put my faith in the leader and only suffered due to his/her ineptitude. Never again! I'm going to control my own destiny."

And with that flip, we can launch another reflexive cycle of under- or over-responsibility. We cause our partners to

FIGURE 1.4   The Cycle of Over-/Under-Responsibility

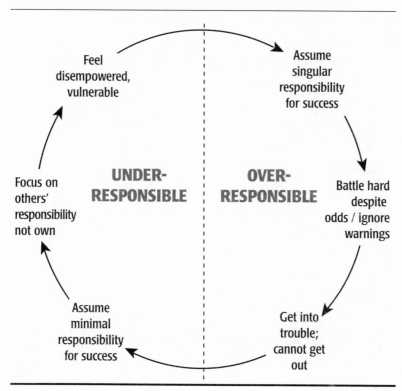

migrate to the opposite extreme and we set ourselves up for failure lurking over the horizon.

Back at *Wapshot*, Michael is so frustrated by weak results that he splits Caroline's job in half. "She's just not as strong as I thought she was when I hired her," Michael rationalizes. "If I cut her job down to size, maybe she can handle it." He hires another advertising vice president, Dieter, to take over the other part of what used to be Caroline's responsibilities. Several months later Michael backs out of his role in advertising sales and declares the responsibility to be fully in the hands of the two vice presidents, who will either perform as directed or be fired.

Caroline, frustrated by a sense of failure and by Michael's stance toward her, takes responsibility for her portion of the advertising sales role, but distances herself completely from Michael and any help he could provide. She throws herself into the task of producing results head down, with blind determination, but she continues to struggle. Having no idea how to perform better on her own, she once again thinks about quitting, and she starts exploring other opportunities on the side.

Dieter is a well-regarded sales executive from a very large magazine company. He is considerably older than Michael and quiet by comparison. More of a "corporate guy," he's used to a high level of supporting infrastructure and lots of perks. He's never operated in a magazine that was not the strongest in its category. Almost immediately his efforts meet with frustration and his progress falls behind plan.

Michael admonishes him to start producing. He can't understand why Dieter is taking such a laid-back attitude to the job at hand.

After only four months on the job, Dieter resigns. His abrupt departure is particularly embarrassing for Michael because he has trumpeted Dieter's arrival as a big coup and the harbinger of great sales growth in Dieter's areas of coverage. Dieter's parting comments still ring in his ears: "You micromanage everything here, Michael, from my expense report to how I manage my salespeople. The support functions are ineffective because they can't move a muscle without you. Now you are saying: 'You're on your own,

Dieter. It's all up to you. You had better produce the pages!' No thanks. I'm not going to be set up for failure."

Michael walks into the early-morning meeting with Louis, depressed and defeated. Three months into the new fiscal year, the magazine is already guaranteed to be off budget. Caroline has failed him completely and checked out emotionally. Little does he know she's really out the door, and that his own replacement is already in the wings. Having worked like a horse over the past quarter to rejuvenate advertising sales, all he has to show for his effort is extreme fatigue, and the first failure of his career.

CHAPTER 2

Role of the
Fear of Failure

Jerry sits alone in the corner office of the headquarters of
Global Products Corporation mulling over the call he has
just received from Chuck, an equity analyst.

Jerry is in his thirty-fifth year with GPC and his fifth as
its CEO. He's a personable man with deep blue eyes and a
wide smile. But right now his mouth is drawn down in
deep concern. Chuck has been a positive voice on the
street for GPC over the past decade, but his call was a
heads up that the "natives were getting restless." Chuck
and his colleagues had become accustomed to GPC churn-
ing out growth on top of growth on top of growth. Few
corporations could match GPC's record of innovation,
customer service, and global market penetration, as well as
its rising sales and profits. In recent years, however, the
mighty GPC growth machine has been slowing down.
Chuck's call was to say that even he was on the verge of

lowering his GPC rating from a buy to a hold because of the weak prospects.

The slowing sales growth is a mystery to Jerry, given their current health and especially the profit picture. However, when Jerry thinks hard about recent initiatives undertaken across the corporation's eight divisions, he realizes that they seem less inspiring, less aggressive, less breakthrough-oriented than the initiatives of previous decades.

He recalls strategy meetings with the divisional presidents and their management teams. As Jerry listened to division after division, he found himself increasingly underwhelmed. Their strategic plans all made sense, but there was little creative, out-of-the-box thinking. And when he offered suggestions on how to improve the plans, the suggestions were treated as attacks to be parried, not ideas to be explored. He pushed for more aggressive plans, but what he got back were revised versions that looked suspiciously like the originals.

Though famously slow to anger, Jerry gets perilously close to the boiling point as he sits and thinks about this new threat—the downgrade from the analysts. What good are strategy meetings when all his people seem to want is a rubber stamp for mediocrity? Real leadership is unwelcome, especially admonitions to stretch and grow. He knows his people are capable of much more, but he also knows they're not even trying. This is unacceptable! He spent the last thirty-five years giving the company 100 percent. He won't tolerate less from anyone else.

He calls the division presidents together to share the analysts' concerns. He tells his team that he's promised to double the rate of sales growth starting next fiscal year and that he's taking personal responsibility for the new goal.

The division presidents listen politely but don't say much, viewing all this with jaundiced eyes. Their approach to strategy sessions has always been "Get in and get out." In their view, they have their hands full delivering the existing profit goals.

After the big meeting, Bob, one of the presidents, sits down with his senior VP, Walter, and explains Jerry's new goal. Walter says that he will try his best but can't promise anything. "I don't have the resources to go after more aggressive growth," he says. Bob nods and says, "Give it your best shot." He empathizes with Walter. What does Jerry want? You can't get blood from a stone!

Once back with his own team, Walter dutifully creates a New Business Ventures group to pursue the new target. To head this NBV slot he picks one of his lieutenants, but not exactly his right-hand man. Despite all this talk, Walter knows that his real job is to run his existing business, and he plans to stick to his knitting.

"I was only a year or two away from a division president slot myself," he grouses. "But now this is going to muddy the water. My business just can't deliver that kind of growth."

Failure often begets failure. In fact, as we saw at *Wapshot, fear of failure* actually helps produce the very failure that we fear. We all know what anxiety can do when it takes hold. Worry too much about an exam and your mind goes blank. Worry too much about spilling a hot cup of coffee and your hand starts to shake, which causes you to spill the cup.

No one wants to get burned, but why do we fear failure to the extent that we do? Why do Bob and Walter not even try to meet Jerry's goals, even though inaction appears to guarantee failure for their company?

It's personal, very personal. But at the same time, it's universal.

Chris Argyris, professor emeritus at Harvard Business School, has delineated what he calls the *governing values* behind most human interactions.[1] These values are like source code in a computer operating system, guiding the way we interpret and deal with our world. They apply to people across ages, cultures, genders, economic status, and educational levels. These governing values are:

- To *win and not lose* in any interaction;
- To always *maintain control* of the situation at hand;
- To *avoid embarrassment* of any kind; and
- To *stay rational* throughout.

For example, if I'm guided by these values in trying to explain to a colleague why I prefer my plan to his, I will try to maintain a conversation in which:

- I convince him that my plan is a better course of action than his plan;
- We stick to my agenda throughout the conversation and don't go off on tangents or get into a big argument;
- We don't have an embarrassing discussion concerning the fact that my point of view prevailed over his; and
- I stay rational throughout, focusing on the logical, not emotional elements of the case.

Over time, we become very skilled in designing all our interactions with others so as to avoid violating these governing values, even though the cost may be outcomes we don't like.

In the conversation I described above, my colleague may come away feeling unheard. He may feel he's been railroaded, and he may avoid working with me in the future. This would not be my intent, but it is a far too likely outcome of operating according to the governing values.

Together, the four governing values combine in us to amplify the fear of failure. The *win-don't-lose* value deals with failure per se—*losing* is failure. And if we fail, others may change their assessment of and shift responsibility away from us in order to avoid a repeated failure. If someone else is given control going forward, that violates the second value—*maintain control.* And any failure, as it violates values one and two, can be humiliating. Thus failure also violates the third value—*avoiding embarrassment.* And finally, failure, loss of control, and embarrassment are likely to force emotions to the surface, violating the fourth value—*staying rational,* staying strictly within the logical structure of the argument and keeping out potentially dangerous emotional features.

When we're operating from the governing values, failure looms so large as a threat that we try to avoid it at almost any cost. When we can't avoid it, we try to cover it up or deny it.

The flood of fear that we experience at the prospect of failure actually short-circuits our conscious, deliberative thought process—ironically the very rationality we seek to maintain—and drives us toward "fight or flight." This response is so primitive that it actually predates the evolution of our brain's prefrontal cortex, the location of higher reasoning. Fight or flight belongs to a separate, pre-rational part of our nervous system located in the brain stem, a structure we inherited from our pre-human, and even pre-mammalian ancestors. Back this far on the evolutionary scale, the emotions are raw, not subtle, and all about basic survival. That's why fear so easily flows into rage. The two share the same chemistry and the same pathways in the brain. They are also hardwired with a direct link to all the systems needed for an immediate, sometimes violent, reaction. So when fear—even the fear of losing a sale or getting a bad performance review—jump-starts this system, it takes over, tensing our muscles, making our hearts pound, and flooding us with stress hormones such as adrenalin. All of this drowns out that small, rational voice located in the prefrontal cortex, that separate and more modern part that you employ when you "use your head."

Confronted by failure itself or the fearful anticipation of failure, we rush to one of two options: 1) *fight*, meaning that we seize total responsibility for the situation; or 2) *flight*, meaning that we assume almost no responsibility for it.

Operating under the tyranny of the governing values, when I resort to the fight response I seek *to win* in the face of failure or acute fear of failure by stretching my level of responsibility, but often significantly above my capabilities. This ensures that I will be in control of my own destiny and, ideally, able to work my way out of the fear-inducing challenges. My desire *to maintain control* causes me to assume full responsibility for the situation, to pre-empt anyone else from seizing control. *To avoid embarrassment*, I assume responsibility without discussion with others, since broaching the subject might expose my underlying belief that others are incompetent and might subject my judgment to critical testing through questioning by others that may highlight my own incompetence. Discussion with others would have the further drawback of becoming emotional, making it difficult for me to *stay rational.*

High intelligence, even membership in a highly rational and deliberative profession, has nothing to do with it. Studies of actual practices among psychologists[2] suggest that, despite their lip service to the logic of argumentation, open dialogue, and critical testing—the scientific method—scientists are just as eager to shield their theories and models from critical testing as are many of the highly rational and deliberative managers that Chris Argyris and I have been studying for years.

Under the tyranny of the governing values, collaboration is dangerous, something to be avoided. If I work in partnership with someone else, the other person may screw up, which would make me part of a losing effort. In a partnership I'm no longer in control. Worse, I may have to be part of all sorts of potentially embarrassing conversations that I would love to avoid.

When I act unilaterally, I tell myself that I am avoiding discussion of my strategy to protect the others from feeling embarrassed. But really, I'm trying to protect myself from awkward conversations with others regarding my dubious qualifications for taking on excessive responsibility, and from establishing explicit and measurable accountability. In effect, I am acting to try to protect myself from failure, while at the same time tacitly holding others responsible for needing the over-protection, despite the fact that they never asked for the protection in the first place.

I call the fight reaction the Al Haig strategy. In the wake of the assassination attempt on President Ronald Reagan, his secretary of state, Alexander Haig, famously announced from the White House, "I'm in charge here." Unfortunately for Secretary Haig, the Constitution actually places the secretary of state fourth in line for responsibility during a presidential crisis. His unilateral assertion of control became fodder for stand-up comics for years.

In the case of GPC, Jerry became fearful when the analysts began to harangue him about the lack of growth. He worried that he would be the first "non-winning" CEO of GPC in decades if the view evolved that during his reign the company stopped growing. He knew Wall Street well enough to recognize that if the analysts were not placated, they could agitate the board and he might lose control of the agenda. All of the above would be intensely and thoroughly embarrassing to him and the corporation and would set the emotions of everyone boiling. All four governing values were at risk.

Jerry's primitive survival instincts took over when his fear reached a threshold level. They triggered the automatic and irrational fight-or-flight response, from which menu Jerry chose to fight. He declared a bold growth goal without consulting his key managers for their input, and without a plan for how to achieve it. He publicly took on full personal responsibility for achieving the goal, even though he had no ability to accomplish it himself. He sought to win, to take control of the winning process, and, by asserting this unilateral control, to avoid any embarrassing conversations about the problems the company faced.

But collaboration can be dangerous from the opposite perspective as well. If I work in partnership with a more dominant person, I won't be in control but I'll be implicated, which, if we lose, becomes a double whammy. To enter a meaningful collaboration, I will have to reveal the degree to which I am scared and worried, and that would be profoundly embarrassing. So collaboration is a threat I prefer to flee.

When I choose the flight response to fear, I withdraw from a responsible stance in order to set the bar low enough to ensure *victory*. I aspire to manage a sufficiently narrowly defined, doable task to keep fully *in control*. By withdrawing, I avoid any situation that would reveal, to my *embarrassment*, that I am not up to the task at hand. In fact, by withdrawing unilaterally I also avoid an embarrassing discussion about my decision to withdraw in the first place. And I avoid the appearance of becoming emotional, thus appearing to *stay rational*, even though my entire constellation of reactions is anything but.

At GPC, Bob and the other division presidents, along with Walter and the other senior VPs, chose flight. This is not surprising given the culture at GPC, which is highly perfectionist. Those who make the grade have always done well and are internally driven to avoid mistakes or failures. They are likely to be their own worst critics, anticipating the criticism of superiors before it arrives.

This perfectionism drives them to place a very high value on dependable outcomes. Fear prompts them to play it safe, and they have great difficulty managing ambiguous situations. They are least fearful when given a clear goal for which they are singularly responsible and for which the likelihood of success is relatively high. Conversely, they are most fearful when they must manage a complex situation in which the goals are conflicting or unclear and the potential for failure is meaningful.

Thus, Bob, Walter, and their colleagues faced a scary bind when presented with the sales growth challenge:

> On one hand, they could explicitly and publicly commit to aggressive sales-growth goals for their own businesses. However, by doing so, they would increase the chance of failing to meet the goals and would risk both personal embarrassment and the potential for disproportionate punishment.
>
> On the other hand, they could explicitly and publicly renounce the setting of aggressive sales-growth goals for their businesses. However, by doing so, they risked being

seen as unleaderly and therefore as failures, producing both personal embarrassment and a threat to further advancement.

Seeking narrow perfectionism is a recognizable variation of the flight response. It's a passive strategy that entails redefining and narrowing the challenge faced so as to assure a successful outcome. It consists of either:

- Acknowledging the existence of an aggressive goal, but delegating the most complex and difficult problems elsewhere—typically, but not exclusively, downward—in order to insulate one's self from the potential for failure; or
- Avoiding acknowledging the existence of an aggressive goal, and redefining victory against more doable criteria.

At GPC, widespread use of the coping strategies of narrow perfectionism produced big problems. The delegation of complexity downward from more senior managers to more junior managers ensured that ever-less-capable managers were given the hardest problems to solve. At the same time, the narrow definition of victory created an environment in which problems were tackled in an incremental fashion and matching incremental solutions were found rather than broad or bold solutions.

The "Al Haig/fight" and the "narrow perfectionism/ flight" reactions to the threat of failure are common across organizations. Both reactions reinforce the previously discussed inability for groups to share responsibility in order to put all of their talents to work solving a problem, but the problem is different in each case.

The narrow perfectionist chops the whole task into parts to produce a piece for which he or she can take responsibility and have reasonable certainty about succeeding. While success is likely to be assured in their small piece, the very act of breaking apart the holistic challenge can make failure on the larger challenge almost certain.

By handing off the growth assignment to a so-so manager in a cordoned-off new ventures group, Walter may succeed in managing his own core business while failing to contribute to the necessary growth in GPC overall. The dilemma for Walter is that if he were to take note of the shortcomings of his new ventures manager and offer to think through his challenge with him, he would be at risk of being implicated in the very failure he fears. Thus the safest way for Walter to deal with the threat posed by the raised growth objective is to distance himself from thinking about it and working on it—which is exactly what he does. And in fact his new ventures manager and most others in GPC fail to produce the targeted growth.

Most CEOs see and complain bitterly about the symptoms of narrow perfectionism in their organizations. They often complain of *functional silos, isolationism,* and *incremental thinking.* In fact, these are all forms of narrow perfectionism in which the pressing challenges of the day are not honestly and forthrightly addressed. And they are not addressed because the Responsibility Virus causes people to avoid collaborating on difficult tasks in which a significant possibility of failure exists.

The Al Haig response creates a different problem. By seizing the whole task alone, the would-be hero maintains the integrity of the challenge rather than chopping it into disintegrated pieces—which is good. However, at the same time, he or she takes on the challenge alone instead of leveraging the skills and capabilities of others who could help with the task—which is bad. It is particularly destructive when, as in the case of Jerry, the CEO, the task lies far beyond his personal capabilities to accomplish. Because the task is seized alone, others tend to step back and let the "heroic" figure do what he will, even as he begins to buckle under the burden.

The narrow perfectionism response produces success on the largely irrelevant component tasks but destroys the integrity of the task. The Al Haig response maintains the integrity of the task but produces a holistic failure. In both cases, real collaboration never enters the picture. Individuals, motivated by their governing values and their fear of failure, work largely alone on tasks that, by their very nature, demand the marshalling of many diverse talents and perspectives.

The Enron debacle, as mentioned earlier, provides an excellent example of narrow perfectionism, along with the Al Haig response, working in concert to produce an epic disaster. While Kenneth Lay assured all that he was in charge and would, in effect, ensure that outside shareholders and employee-shareholders would continue to enrich themselves off Enron, numerous other folks played the narrow perfectionism game. Financiers defined victory as getting Enron its money and nothing more. Ensuring that the interests of the providers of the capital were protected, for example, was not a consideration. Auditors defined victory as ensuring that Enron complied with the letter of the law and nothing more. Lawyers defined victory as providing an opinion that it was all right to shred documents—not, for example, whether it was ethical to shred documents. The board defined victory as making sure it was protected by the opinions of auditors and lawyers and nothing more—not, for example, whether the firm was risking everything. The fear of failure that helped drive each player to narrow its sights helped produce results worse than any failure they could have predicted.

Back at GPC, a year after making his growth pronouncement, Jerry sits at his desk feeling quite alone. Sales growth has actually slowed instead of speeding up. The analysts are writing ever more inflammatory reports referring to the "anemic" performance at GPC. The lack of progress internally has him frustrated. Nothing has changed in the past year; the strategy meetings still feel like Muhammad Ali's "rope-a-dope." He feels as if he were punching at fog! New venture groups have sprung up everywhere, but they seem to be second-class citizens when it comes to resources and attention. Everybody seems to be declaring victory on his or her small piece of turf, but it all adds up to failure for GPC. The analysts want to know how he's going to meet his five-year sales growth target given that Year One was so miserable. "Miserable?" he says to himself. "What's their problem? If you look at profits, we set a record."

"Maybe we need to try something even more radical," he mutters. "Maybe if I can't fix this, somebody else should try."

CHAPTER 3

Static and Dynamic Conservation of Responsibility

The International Development Agency is perhaps the world's most elite economic development agency. It is full of bright and superbly educated professionals, cosmopolitan and committed, from around the globe.

Pierre, a handsome thirty-five-year-old, fluent in seven languages, able to hold his own in almost any conversation, is typical. He finished at the top of his class as an undergraduate in his native France, and then went on to graduate school in North America, financed by a full scholarship, to study development economics. In his final year of study, every investment bank in New York and London plied him with offers, but he was more interested in a career of public service, working to overcome Third World poverty.

Pierre spent two years in introductory training and, upon completion of the program, was assigned to Africa as a development officer. There he worked primarily on IDA projects designed to improve power and transportation. IDA's theory was that without basic infrastructure, these African economies were incapable of progress. The projects, however, required massive amounts of capital, took many years to reach fruition, and, to date, had been limited in their effectiveness.

After four years of exemplary work, Pierre was offered a position in the newly formed Private Sector Development Unit. The PSDU had been created to bring together the best and brightest professionals from across IDA to deliver complex services to Third World clientele. Joining this elite group was an offer he could not refuse, and a dedicated and enthusiastic Pierre leapt to the challenge.

"I'm smart, well-educated, and I've been around the block a time or two," he tells himself. "I know what doesn't work, and I have a pretty good idea what will work. With the flexibility provided by this new mandate, I can create innovative new lending programs that provide more sophisticated help than these big infrastructure projects. Given what I've learned already, I can ensure the quality of these loans and protect the agency's viability. However, I can't expect a great deal of help from officials in the borrower countries, because they don't have my level of skill and insight. And the agency people outside the PSDU are pretty conservative, so I can't expect much there either. But that's OK, because I can carry the ball; in fact it is my duty. I simply have to be diplomatic with the borrowing country officials and not let them think I'm driving this process."

Pierre's first PSDU undertaking is an integrated project to develop an industrial sector of the Cameroonian economy. He works hard on the initiative, creating a detailed financial plan and implementation with a breathtaking level of documentation. He asks for no help or support from his agency colleagues. When he feels confident that he has all the bases covered, he asks his immediate superior for permission to go to Cameroon with the proposal. His boss, thinking there is little downside, gives quick approval without reviewing the proposal in detail.

Pierre travels to Cameroon to meet with Hakeem, the key official who is the point person on the African side. Hakeem is certainly friendly enough. A somewhat portly man in his mid-fifties, Hakeem laughs uproariously when, toward the end of the first day's session, Pierre suggests that they work through dinner. "My young friend," chuckles Hakeem, "we have to put some food in front of you because when you eat will be the only time you will stop talking." In fact, Hakeem has already picked out a favorite restaurant, a place with great local delicacies and lovely ambience. Pierre enjoys the food but is a little put off by Hakeem's refusal to talk about the project over dinner. They plow through numerous courses and bottles of wine. Then the dinner breaks up and Pierre heads back to the hotel to prepare for the next day's meeting.

By 10 a.m. the following day, Pierre is truly annoyed. Though the meeting was scheduled at 9 a.m., Hakeem is nowhere to be seen, and no one seems to know his whereabouts. At 11:45 the Cameroonian walks in, apologizes modestly, and settles down at his desk. Pierre recaps the previous day's meeting and completes his presentation. Though Pierre is pleased with how well his ideas have come together, he is disappointed with Hakeem's reaction. Pierre assumed that he would jump on board. But instead of expressing gratitude for Pierre's hard work and leadership, Hakeem begins imposing constraints. He objects to performance conditions—such as a monitoring agency to prevent graft and corruption on the project—that Pierre and the agency attach to the funding of any project.

Undaunted, Pierre forges ahead, making modifications to the proposal based on Hakeem's concerns. He meets again with Hakeem to outline his revisions, and then he asks Hakeem for the work that he'd promised to undertake coming out of their last meeting. Hakeem has nothing to show, but appears not the least embarrassed by this failure to deliver. In addition, he voices still more objections and concerns about the project. "Talk about ingratitude!" Pierre mutters to himself, as he packs to leave. "And they're jeopardizing internal agency approval with all their roadblocks. Now I've got to worry about both the borrower approval and the agency approval. I've really got my work cut out for me."

Once back at the agency, Pierre tries to devise a compromise plan. In his view, the agency needs to soften its stance on a couple of issues and work with him to convince Hakeem that Cameroon, too, must show some flexibility. Pierre reviews the situation with his superior, but to his dismay and disappointment, he is informed that the agency position is firm. "Best of luck," he is told, "in getting the Cameroonians to agree to the agency conditions."

Pierre returns to his office steaming with anger. "I'm trying to help these people. I'm trying to save the agency from its most conservative tendencies, and nobody lifts a finger to help me! What's their problem? Who do they think is going to help them? Zorro? The Green Hornet?"

In subsequent meetings and in written communications, Pierre is sharper and more extreme with Hakeem. Hakeem, weary of Pierre's pressure, stops inviting him to meetings.

Pierre throws up his hands in despair. Already angered and disillusioned by Third World leaders, he now feels betrayed by his own agency. He consoles himself by thinking: "It's not my fault; it's theirs. Anyway, it is not my country. It was all for them, but the Cameroonians wouldn't step up to the plate, so too bad."

When Hakeem calls to ask when Pierre will return with the updated proposal, Pierre lowers the boom. There will be no project, he says. Hakeem, who until this point in the whole process has been lighthearted and jovial, thinks that the until-now humorless Pierre has mustered his first joke. "No, I'm deadly serious," Pierre says. This sends Hakeem into a rage. "How can you do this? We were counting on the IDA money. We just had a few wrinkles to work out. We've already started spending on the project, expecting your funds. Now we will have to stop and our budget will be in deficit. You aren't here to help but to be the imperialists who have always terrorized us."

Pierre is stunned by the reaction. He apologizes curtly and hangs up the phone. "I know we've got to do better to stay relevant as a global organization, but this place will never change," he tells himself. "If this is the only thanks I'm going to get for trying to save the world, I might as well go be a Wall Street investment banker."

Determined to protect himself from further disappointment, Pierre concentrates on doable tasks, primarily the drafting of long technical reports. He lapses into an increasingly cynical state as he deals with the loss of his idealism. He feels so undone by the agency bureaucracy that he now begins to doubt its basic commitment. He wonders whether he was foolish and naive to give up a lucrative career in order to help ungrateful and lazy Third World countries. He watches in despair as the agency comes under increasing external attack for being ineffective and hidebound.

Long experience with relationships such as that between Pierre and Hakeem tells me that there is a relatively fixed amount of responsibility to be assumed in any situation, and that any amount of over-responsibility is offset by an equal amount of under-responsibility.

In this way, the Responsibility Virus operates according to a law I call the Conservation of Responsibility. The name is borrowed from thermodynamics, where the First Law states that energy in a closed system is neither created nor destroyed. If I strike a billiard ball with a cue, the energy I put into thrusting the cue forward is transferred into the ball, which causes it to move forward. All the energy is transferred into the momentum of the ball (except for a bit that is dissipated in heat energy where the cue strikes it).

We can speak of two different kinds of Conservation of Responsibility:

- Static conservation between two individuals at a given point in time, and
- Dynamic conservation in a single individual over the course of time.

Together, static and dynamic conservation of responsibility account for most of the damage created by the Responsibility Virus.

Static Conservation of Responsibility

Pierre enters the Cameroonian scenario with a mindset common to the young professionals at the PSDU, a point of view that I call *Save the World*.

Pierre's stance is noble. He genuinely wants his impoverished client to prosper and he puts everything he has into the effort of making this happen. The sting of previous failures at the agency spurs him on. However, his passion and enthusiasm push him to assume complete responsibility for success, despite the extreme difficulty of the challenge. He will make all the critical choices himself, without assistance or consultation. Importantly, he asks for nothing in return but passive cooperation from both the remainder of the agency and the Cameroonian officials. He sees no merit in collaboration in making the key choices. In fact, danger lurks in collaboration. Less talented colleagues at the Agency or self-interested Cameroonians may dilute the strength and wisdom of his program.

Without realizing it, Pierre is sending Hakeem and the Cameroonians a signal: *I am the hero! Stand aside and be saved.* Hakeem recognizes that in order to take a greater share of the responsibility for the project, he would have to seize it back from Pierre, a powerful person backed by the powerful IDA. Given Pierre's enthusiasm, this is a daunting challenge Hakeem would rather avoid.

Hakeem's reaction illustrates the first law of thermodynamics as applied to responsibility. To the degree that Pierre acts over-responsibly, Hakeem takes on an equal and opposite level of under-responsibility.

In many years spent working with organizations, I have only rarely seen the individual in Hakeem's position fight to push the other actor toward a more balanced collaboration. Typically, the Hakeem character also remembers the sting of some prior failure and is not eager to insist on more responsibility. Because Pierre discusses neither the fact that he is taking on the lion's share of the responsibility, nor why he has taken this step (both would bring on embarrassment, in violation of the governing value), Hakeem is left to his own interpretation of Pierre's words and actions. He reads Pierre's behavior, in this case rightly, as a vote of no confidence in Hakeem's capabilities and as a clear signal that he doesn't want Hakeem as a collaborating partner.

So Hakeem accedes and becomes passive. In mirror form, he does so without discussion, because discussion would be embarrassing and might place him in a losing position—both violations of governing principles. Hakeem's passivity convinces Pierre that his doubts about Hakeem's capabilities and attitudes are accurate. And with that conviction, the Virus is running rampant. The first steps by Pierre—coming to Hakeem with a fully baked proposal and plan—and by Hakeem—taking on a passive stance from the outset—are the initial outbreak, and they foreshadow more extreme positions of over- and under-responsibility to come.

Hakeem and the Cameroonian officials slip quickly into a dependent mode each time the over-responsible Pierre and his staff arrive. They hold Pierre and the agency disproportionately responsible for delays in the project and lack of improvement in the conditions they face.

Pierre does not seek assistance from or share responsibility with the Cameroonian officials, which fuels his frustration with their lack of participation and leads him to treat the Cameroonians with increasing contempt. Although Pierre uses the best of his diplomatic training in an attempt to hide it, his lack of respect reads through. In the face of his belittling behavior, which they don't fully understand, the Cameroonians sit back, make demands, and pile the work higher on Pierre's plate. They slip into a highly under-responsible stance in which they have little regard for or even interest in Pierre's difficulties and challenges.

In parallel, Pierre treats the agency departments charged with approving various aspects of the program as obstacles to be overcome, not as valuable collaborators. In response, they tire quickly of his overbearing attitude. Having no sense of investment in the success of the project, the internal IDA approval agents stick close to the letter of the internal regulations, playing the role of bureaucrats to the hilt.

At every juncture, and fully in keeping with the principle of *static conservation*, Pierre's actions unwittingly encourage greater under-responsibility from the other parties:

The Cameroonians' initial reaction to his complete proposal is passivity.

Pierre's reaction to the passivity is to seize still more responsibility and show contempt for the under-responsible Cameroonians.

The Cameroonians' response to the contempt is to cede even more responsibility.

Pierre's reaction is to seize still more responsibility, and so on.

He follows a similar pattern with his colleagues in the agency.

In both scenarios, the parties take an initial step from the middle ground that would be consistent with their capabilities; Pierre takes on duties beyond his abilities, while the Cameroonians and the agency step down from what they are capable of achieving.

Dynamic Conservation of Responsibility

When, at the point of despair, Pierre flips dramatically over to a new stance, the *Do the Best I Can* stage, he illustrates perfectly the *dynamic conservation of responsibility*. In this stance, Pierre sees other parties as almost exclusively responsible for the failure. Narrow-minded agency departments, self-interested and/or lazy bureaucrats in the borrowing country, world economic trends, plus anything else that comes to mind, are the forces to blame for the failure, not Pierre. While each of his criticisms may hold a kernel of truth, Pierre apportions far too much responsibility to the other parties and too little to himself.

The *dynamic conservation of responsibility* holds that, by acting over-responsibly, we build up what might be thought of as a responsibility surplus, or, by acting under-responsibly, a responsibility deficit. These surpluses and deficits balance over time.

While the surplus (for example, for Pierre) or deficit (for example, for Hakeem) is building up, the force of *static conservation* pushes us further and further from the balance point as described above. Pierre becomes more and more over-responsible, Hakeem more and more under-responsible.

Eventually the mismatches between responsibility and capability force some traumatic event. When we are over-responsible, our trauma is typically a crushing failure, like that of the Cameroonian project, from which it is difficult to distance ourselves.

Similarly, when we are under-responsible, the triggering event is likely to be a crushing blow to the seeming safety and stability of our dependent stance. For Hakeem, the crushing blow came when the IDA announced that the Cameroonian project had been permanently shelved and its priorities were being refocused elsewhere. Hakeem had been certain that Pierre would eventually prevail and that the conditions that he had imposed on the project could and indeed would be met by the agency. Now he faced a future with no hard-driving Pierre, no IDA, no project, but all the poverty and despair with which he started. And since he was betting that the project would go forward, he had already spent some of the money! Failure doesn't often get more embarrassing than that.

The sad irony is that when the traumatic moment brought on by the static conservation of responsibility manifests itself, neither party migrates to a balanced position. The over-responsible individual, powered by the momentum of a responsibility surplus, tends to flip all the way to under-responsibility, saying, "I tried the best I could; it was just an impossible task." The under-responsible party, fueled by an angry reaction to being let down and subjected to pain and/or humiliation, flips all the way to over-responsibility, saying, "I trusted them, and they let me down; now I have to take complete care of myself."

The greater the cumulative level of responsibility surplus/deficit, the greater is the magnitude of the flip over to the other side. The greater the mismatch, the more catastrophic and traumatic is the result. The more traumatic the result, the greater is the overreaction.

Social psychologists see flips in the assignment of responsibility as a species of "ego-preserving biases."[1] Participants in experiments often make what are called attributions when trying to explain their own failures. "I tripped while dancing" gets rationalized as "it was dark and the floor was wet." For the owner of the room, "Johnny tripped while dancing" becomes "Johnny wasn't paying attention."

For Pierre, the trauma of failure in Cameroon drives him deep into an under-responsible mode. His long technical reports—essentially busy work—reveal his newfound cynicism. He succeeds only by setting the bar so low that he can't fail. He avoids making bad choices by making simple choices only, and as few of them as possible. He expresses a strong feeling of being a pawn in the hands of the agency, the client countries, and life in general. Those around him remember the old Pierre and whisper about his burnout. They assume that he won't do anything valuable, so they don't give him important projects.

Pierre's under-responsibility does not last forever, however. In due course, he becomes frustrated with his own cynicism and feelings of disempowerment. The doable tasks, the easy but unimportant work, start to weigh on him, as does the external criticism of the agency. As a result, Pierre becomes inspired to try anew. "I'm going to fundamentally change the way the agency does business," he determines. He decides to take on the internal bureaucrats who stand in the way of progress. Sadly, this new definition of responsibility merely flips Pierre back into the realm of the undoable, which again sets the stage for disappointment, to be followed by his next bout of passivity.

Meanwhile, back in Cameroon, Hakeem rails against the capricious and unreliable international agencies and swears never again to allow Cameroon to be in their sway. "We can do this sort of work ourselves and go directly to private sector banks for funding. They are more reliable and will be impressed with our initiative." In due course, Hakeem discovers that getting rid of all the international development agencies and going it alone is beyond his capacity and that the private banks have their own reliability challenges. He fails, and in the wake of the failure returns to a passive stance in which he turns over leadership to development agencies once again.

Static and Dynamic Conservation
of Responsibility in Concert

Taken together, *static and dynamic conservation* create a system in which we are perpetually held in an unbalanced state. *Static conservation* lures us away from a level of responsibility consistent with our capability. *Dynamic conservation* takes hold as we build up a cumulative responsibility surplus or deficit and—powered by failure—flings us across to the other extreme. This helps us balance our surplus or deficit, but puts us in the position of creating a new imbalance, since we have been flung to a new point of over- or under-responsibility.

Pierre and his colleagues typically came to the PSDU and entered on the *Save the World* side. In due course, they experienced failure and flipped to *Do the Best I Can*. However, this didn't last either. Eventually they flipped back, only to flip again.

The interaction between *static and dynamic conservation of responsibility* makes the Responsibility Virus a self-reinforcing, not self-correcting, loop. Once the Virus gets started, we find it extremely hard to fight because *static conservation* creates the surplus/deficit on which *dynamic conservation* feeds. *Dynamic conservation* in turn drives the swing that creates the next surplus/deficit, and so on. . . .

The Responsibility Virus produces a succession of traumatic failures, which in turn causes a range of significant long-term problems for organizations and the individuals composing them. It destroys the capacity for collaboration, and then creates an atmosphere of mistrust and misunderstanding. Ultimately, it leads to the atrophy of choice-making skills.

FIGURE 3.1   The Cycle of Over-/Under-Responsibility at the IDA

"Save the World"

- Self-fulfilling outcomes
- Cynicism and disempowerment reinforced

- Set profound change, high-quality loans as only valid goal
- Expect borrowers and rest of agency to help me / see things my way

- Concentrate on doable tasks (e.g., tech. reports)
- Share views privately with colleagues
- Norms keep views undiscussable in public

UNDER-RESPONSIBLE

OVER-RESPONSIBLE

- Feel responsible for loan quality, changing borrowers, making $ for agency
- Advocate my view; fight to win

- Not my fault; it's theirs
- Not my country
- It's undoable
- This place will never change

- Rest of agency won't do what I want; impasse is not resolved in my favor
- Little development and poverty reduction
- I give in / give up

"Do the Best I Can"

PART 2

Costs of the Responsibility Virus

CHAPTER 4

The Death
of Collaboration

Willem was a CEO both quick and skillful at decision-making, an intuitive manager. Still, he had no idea what to make of the call he'd just received from Hong Kong. Kenny, his favorite regional president, was on the line complaining about how the organizational structure of the firm, DevTek, impeded his ability to manage his business and win in Asia. Willem had heard much grousing before about the structure, but it all came from managers he saw as whiners. Kenny *never* complained. Willem had to take his concerns seriously.

He buzzed his secretary to cancel his next meeting and to bring him a fresh cup of coffee. Then he leaned back and tried to figure out what the hell to make of this.

DevTek had started as a German company, organized by function. Everybody in the organization reported to the VP of marketing, or the VP of manufacturing, or the VP of

sales or of R&D or operations, and each of these VPs reported to the CEO. As DevTek grew, like other expanding
firms it seemed to outgrow the functional structure. It became increasingly confusing for the same VP of R&D to
juggle the very different needs of six increasingly diverse
product lines, everything from valves and fittings to foam
insulation. DevTek established a new structure in which
there was a managing director (MD) for each of the six
product lines, with full profit responsibility and reporting
directly to the CEO. In this structure, the functional
groups—marketing, sales, R&D—supported the six MDs
in achieving their profit objectives.

As the firm expanded globally and the international
business grew dramatically, Willem created a new organization with regional presidents in charge of the four regions—North America, Latin America, Europe, and Asia.
The regional structure was seen to be necessary because,
across the regions, the markets were at different stages of
economic development and DevTek penetration. The regional presidents were in charge of developing DevTek's
six product-line businesses in their region through understanding the local customers and enhancing their regional
distribution channels. Perhaps most importantly, now regional presidents—not product-line MDs—were responsible for the bottom line across the six product lines in their
region, with a regional product-line MD reporting to them
in each of the six product lines, and a functional head reporting to them for each of sales, marketing, operations,
R&D, and so forth.

While the regional structure helped DevTek get closer
to its customers around the globe, it left the six product
lines parceled out among four regional presidents, chopping their resources into four pieces, which were not

always well coordinated. While one key competitor managed its valve business as a single integrated global entity supporting that one standard product line around the world, DevTek had slightly different valve products in each of the four regions. The four-part structure caused DevTek to fritter away its research and development money on smaller regional projects.

Still dissatisfied, Willem created an overlay organization charged with coordinating product lines across geographies. These global product-line primes (PLP) had no profit responsibilities or direct line authority over personnel, but they were to create long-term global strategies, which Willem hoped would offset the competitive disadvantages inherent in DevTek's regionalized structure.

It was this new overlay structure that set Kenny off. "It takes so long to get anything done around here," he complained. "Everybody has three bosses. Career progression is dependent on the functional boss. But then they take direct orders from their geographic boss who has profit responsibility for that region. And they now have a PLP from global headquarters telling them not to pay too much attention to the short-term concerns of their regional boss and instead work for the long-term global benefit of the product line, whatever the hell that means!"

Willem knew the current three-way matrix of regional presidents, product-line primes and functional VPs wasn't working. There were too many fights for control, too much ambiguity and confusion. It was time to make a change.

Willem worked with organizational design experts within DevTek and top experts from outside to redesign the structure. He set the goal as creating what he called "single-point accountability."

"Managers need to have one boss, not this complicated matrix," he announced. "We need to know who's in charge in every situation."

The organizational redesign team considered all the options and evaluated them against Willem's goal. They recommended a return to the product-line structure DevTek had enjoyed when it was largely a German, not global, company, but a product-line structure at the global level. Six global managing directors were appointed, reporting directly to Willem, and given profit responsibility for a global product line.

There would be no more confusion about who was in charge at DevTek—the six global MDs would be the point people of single-point accountability.

However, the redesign team realized that having six product-line organizations replicating the in-country operations around the world created confusion in the distribution channels and needless duplication of costs. So they created eight regions, each with a regional development president (DP) responsible for executing the go-to-market strategies of the six global product lines. They were not to interfere with the single-point accountability of the global MDs, but to provide leverage for them.

At first the change was greeted with enthusiasm, especially for the promise of simplification and single-point accountability. However, as managers tried to operate in the new design, they quickly became confused, then angry. They understood the goal and the principle, but global MDs were regularly frustrated with what they saw as lack of cooperation by the regional DPs. Meanwhile, the regional DPs were annoyed that the global MDs didn't appreciate their genuine efforts to create synergies.

Managers saw the new organizational design as being just as complex and confusing as the old one. They began to question what the redesign team actually meant by single-point accountability, when it seemed clear that in practice, at least, the global MDs and the regional DPs had to share responsibility. DevTek's version of single-point accountability seemed such a sham that everyone began to question the design team's sincerity.

When Willem heard the feedback he became more frustrated than ever. "Don't they understand the power of the new structure? It's so much simpler. They just have to get used to it and then they'll get it."

He issued a "flame-mail" to the entire organization, telling them that they had to forget the past and embrace this new simplified organization. Anybody who had a problem with it should speak with him directly.

When Willem's savvy secretary read the e-mail, she knew she wouldn't have to set aside much time for meetings on this subject. And she was right. There weren't many volunteers brave enough to come forward and challenge the new structure.

The first major cost of the Responsibility Virus is that it undermines the capacity for genuine, productive collaboration. Diminished collaboration among employees within the firm means that companies do not benefit from economies of scale as they grow and globalize. Large projects spanning diverse geographies can't be integrated without taming the virus.

The Responsibility Virus also undermines collaboration with other firms, with customers, and with suppliers, each of which is increasingly important as the business world becomes more networked and as the boundaries between internal and external become fuzzier.

Collaboration, by definition, occurs only when two or more individuals *share meaningful* responsibility for producing a choice. *Sharing* means allocating responsibility in rough proportion to each party's choice-making capacity. *Meaningful* implies that the act of sharing the load is important to the outcome: that is, one or the other collaborator could not accomplish the task on a consistent basis without the contribution of the other.

Collaboration occurs when *we're* in charge. It does not occur when *I'm in charge and you're not*, or *you're in charge and I'm not*.

Why is the meaningful sharing of responsibility so difficult? The core culprit is the fear of failure, because, once again, fear rides in on the coattails of the governing values.

Sharing responsibility meaningfully means sharing control, which violates the value *maintain control*. Once responsibility is shared, we can no longer keep control of the recognition and rewards that accrue for winning, so true collaboration runs afoul of the first governing value: *win, don't lose*. Deciding the proper way to apportion responsibilities in a fashion consistent with capabilities can lead to awkward conversations, and thus sharing responsibility violates the third governing value: *avoid embarrassment*. And it can all get emotionally messy, violating the value of *staying rational*. As we saw with Michael and Caroline at *Wapshot*, and with Pierre and Hakeem in Cameroon, it is much easier to divide responsibility unilaterally than to have a potentially embarrassing conversation about it.

Looked at in light of the governing values, collaboration becomes the very embodiment of the threat of failure. In the minds of would-be participants, collaboration is a jungle filled with dangers, any one of which can prompt the fight-or-flight response at any moment. Instead of entering into a discussion about the way to manage the challenge together, the parties decide unilaterally whether to seize responsibility or distance themselves from it. And from their first subtle gesture, they send and pick up signals from the other party that guide and reinforce their actions. In due course, the responsibility is shunted off disproportionately to one party or the other.

Without collaboration, as the complexity of a problem increases, there is no commensurate increase in the capabilities that can be readily applied to it.

Let's say I'm the engineer responsible for designing the composite materials casing for my firm's latest lightweight laptop personal computer. If I'm told halfway through the project that the casing needs to weigh 20 percent less and be 15 percent stronger, I may well be able to rise to the challenge. But if I were told that, in addition, the design must incorporate the embedding of computer circuitry directly into the casing material, I would be out of my depth, because I have no electrical engineering training or experience. I could try to do my design, and then hand it off to the electrical engineering department to do their part. But ideally, my design should take into account the circuitry requirements. So then, perhaps, I might suggest that the electrical engineers do their part first and then hand it to me. But if I'm told that won't work either, then I'm stuck with the need to collaborate with an electrical engineer to solve the difficult design challenge together.

At this point, susceptibility to the Responsibility Virus is very high. The governing values would dictate that either I run the project or an electrical engineer runs th project, and that, as they say, is that. This either/or thinking impairs the capacity of the organization to respond to the challenge.

A large organization may have scores of materials engineers and hundreds of electrical engineers, but that capacity cannot be applied against the particular challenge at hand unless the organization can effect collaboration between an individual materials engineer and an individual electrical engineer. Yet both their inclinations will be to say either "I'm in charge and you're not" or "You're in charge and I'm not."

Inability to collaborate means that individual capabilities are not additive. In terms of effectiveness, when two non-collaborative individuals are assigned to accomplish a task together, 1 + 1 still equals 1, not 2. If Firm A has twice as many people as Firm B, it may be able to handle twice as many simple problems that don't require collaboration. However, unless it can manage true collaboration, it is no more capable of handling complex problems requiring input from multiple employees than is any smaller firm.

In 1793, Adam Smith explained functional specialization in organizations according to the logic of efficiency.[1] In this view, functional specialization of the individual is a good idea because it allows for each person to focus on a single task and derive the benefits of narrow learning-by-doing as it relates to a single function within the broader economy. More recent studies of industrial innovation, however, show that major product-level inventions often come from outside of the firm whose immediate concern is the product itself.[2] Studies of conceptual innovation show also that many ideas come from outside the core discipline that ends up deriving most benefits from them,[3] so the economic logic of specialization does not seem to hold.

An alternative explanation for the logic of specialization is the Responsibility Virus. Each individual wants to limit the scope of his or her activities to a set over which he or she feels wholly responsible, and exclude from this set those activities over which he or she feels not responsible. The collective effect is mass specialization, without the benefits of cross-functional integration and cross-pollination, which will be resisted. This aligns perfectly with the "not-invented-here" syndrome found in so many corporations.

By virtue of the limits it places on the benefits of scale, the Responsibility Virus helps to explain why so many innovative solutions to unmet customer needs come out of small start-ups rather than giant corporations. The inability of employees in large corporations to collaborate successfully is particularly costly in the twenty-first century. As corporations pursue global opportunities, they must leverage scale to succeed. To successfully leverage scale, employees must be able to collaborate. That's the only way they can bring their skills to bear on the challenges associated with the complexity of the global environment.

As DevTek grew from a largely German firm to a truly international firm, it recognized the need to take into account the great differences in the geographic regions. The European approach was ill-suited to Latin America, for example. In addition, since all six of the product lines were distributed largely through the same distribution channels in a given region, there was a compelling rationale for exploiting leverage with the distribution channel across the six product lines. In the context of the regional diversity and the need to leverage in the local distribution channels, it made sense to have strong regional bosses responsible for customizing to optimally suit their region, and for creating leverage with the distribution channel across the six product lines.

However, in a rapidly globalizing market, DevTek needed to leverage its resources for each product line across the globe. Having each product line split into four pieces, each managed by a regional boss who traded off the needs of individual product lines against one another in their region, created inefficiencies relative to truly global competitors. For instance, if the global player had $100 million to invest globally, he might well take advantage of broad opportunities in R&D; the regional player might not see or take advantage of those same opportunities, with four regional managers seeing themselves as spending $25 million each.

Clearly the regional bosses and the global product-line bosses need to collaborate to succeed. The regional aspects and the global aspects have to be considered together to be optimized. But at DevTek, collaboration was not taking place. Both the regional presidents and the product-line primes were frustrated and engaging in counterproductive activities. Instead of attempting to figure out how to work together, they battled over who was in charge. Most of the regional presidents—citing the demands of profit responsibility—declared themselves to be *in charge* and the PLPs to be *not in charge*. As a result, the regional presidents saw the PLPs as rather useless meddlers; the PLPs saw the regional presidents as narrow-minded, self-interested, and imperious. The PLPs held the regional presidents fully responsible for any shortcomings in the business results and the regional presidents, like Kenny, held the structure responsible for their failures. Only a small minority of DevTek regional presidents and PLPs, those with more open attitudes and stronger collaboration skills, made the structure work.

Willem reacted to the counterproductive battling in a characteristic fashion by declaring someone else to be in charge—the new global managing directors—with their "single-point accountability." The old structure was a complicated and confusing matrix in which everyone abdicated responsibility. The new structure, at least in Willem's view, was clear and simplified, one in which nobody could be confused. Global MDs would be in charge and regional development presidents would happily provide leverage.

But this structure simply bypassed the true locus of conflict and created an environment in which the global MDs and regional DPs had little incentive to try to collaborate. Rather, the global MDs had the incentive and the authority to impose their will on the regional DPs. However, such global MD behavior is over-responsible, and regional DP behavior becomes under-responsible in response. The regional aspects were truly important to business success, too, and the six global MDs all needed the support and collaboration of the eight regional DPs. At a time when collaboration was urgently needed, Willem's rhetoric and the structure he imposed provided for just the opposite.

Not surprisingly, the DevTek managers quickly discovered that the new simplified structure was not in fact simple. It merely changed the terms of the conflict, and kept the Responsibility Virus alive and well.

Ineffectiveness in collaboration appears in guises such as "functional silos," "local fiefdoms," or the "not-invented-here syndrome." Regardless of the particular variant, the effect is to reduce to the level of the individual the capacity to take on responsibility for a task. This significantly limits the capacity of the organization to utilize its collective resources.

The same limitations that apply to collaboration within the walls of the organization apply outside the walls as well. The capacity for working together productively with other corporations, often competitors, is increasingly important in the twenty-first-century economy. For example, with Comcast Corporation's purchase of AT&T's cable business, Comcast and AOL Time Warner have the biggest two cable television systems in the United States by far. Each would dearly love to buy the other's system to achieve the scale efficiencies and coverage needed to dramatically enhance cable-delivered features (for example, interactive TV, cable telephony, and cable Internet access). However, neither party has any intention of selling its crown jewel to anyone else, let alone a major competitor. The only way to achieve the value inherent in their cable systems is to collaborate. This would be very difficult for both because each is used to being in charge of all critical parts of its business. Neither company, therefore, would be inclined to be a silent partner or junior partner. Both would be infinitely more comfortable being in charge. To collaborate, they would have to divide responsibility and take joint responsibility for success or failure, something neither is well equipped to do. So the opportunity lies wasting, with the capacity for collaboration remaining the critical barrier.

Similarly, the ability to collaborate outside the walls with customers and suppliers is increasingly important to the success of organizations. The outsourcing of major functions of organizations (such as IT, manufacturing, distribution, and customer service) is one of the major trends of the past ten years. However, the track record of outsourcing is mixed. The Responsibility Virus causes organizations to hold firmly onto functions past the point at which they cease to be best at operating them ("I'm in charge") and then in frustration hand them over to outsourcers and wash their hands ("You're in charge"). As a result, they stand back and judge the outsourcing firm on its performance rather than helping it adjust to changes and improve its service. In due course, performance deteriorates because the outsourcer can't intuit the firm's changing needs without its help.

Firms need to find their way to the "We're in charge" position. In this mode, the firm recognizes that it shares in the responsibility for the success of the function, even though it has contracted for it to be performed by an outside organization, so it retains some responsibility for success. Similarly, the outsourcer understands that it is not completely in charge but rather must depend on the firm to help it understand the evolving needs and the ways to migrate its service over time.

Likewise, firms that collaborate with their customers achieve advantage over those that are either over-responsible or under-responsible. For example, a law firm that faces complaints from its clients about escalating legal costs could take the stance that it is simply the problem of the client (under-responsible) or that it is its own problem and it should reduce rates to clients 10 percent across the board (over-responsible). Both of these approaches are less effective than partnering with the client to explore how legal costs could be reduced through more intelligent use of outside legal services mixed with (for example) selected in-house work.

The obstacle, of course, is that once the collaborative path is initiated, control is compromised, failure cannot be kept at arm's length, and embarrassment may ensue. These are the risks, emotionally difficult to bear, that keep organizations from grasping the benefits not just of collaboration per se, but of the economies of scale for which collaboration is an essential element.

CHAPTER 5

The Development
of Mistrust and
Misunderstanding

Dwight and Harry were both experienced attorneys at White & Jeffries, both members of the executive committee, but the two men could not have been more different. Dwight exuded confidence and competence. He was an always impeccably dressed forty-five-year-old, tall and good looking. And he was a bundle of energy, either fidgeting during long meetings or listening to the conversation while writing a memo on the side. He loved nothing more than leading the charge on a tough, complicated takeover battle. He would look his client in the eye, say "no problem," then work day and night to keep his word. Young lawyers at the firm loved to go into the fray alongside Dwight because they knew their leader was fearless and irrepressible.

In every respect that Dwight was charismatic, Harry was careful. A bookish, slightly rumpled man of fifty-five, he brought a sense of thoroughness and conservatism to his securities work. Clients felt comfortable having Harry on the team because they knew he would cross every *t* and dot every *i*. However, he could annoy them at the beginning of a case with his pessimism, which was only rarely justified. Clients would most likely be told all the bad things that could happen and how a favorable outcome was a long shot. Then Harry would work in a thorough if somewhat plodding manner until he produced an outcome that usually overshot the original prediction. Junior partners and associates dreaded being assigned to Harry's cases because of his dour approach and the intensity with which he controlled their work.

The differences between Dwight and Harry were never sharper than at the most recent executive committee meeting, when the senior partners discussed strategic options for changing the direction of the firm. Dwight thought this meeting was a watershed event, vital to their future. He and several of his senior colleagues felt that W&J had started to drift. They needed to make some tough choices to regain momentum in a tough marketplace for legal services.

But Harry was having none of it. At the meeting, he stood with those saying this was no time for radical change.

"Sure," Dwight thought as he left the conference room and walked back to his office. "That's exactly what he would say given who he is. Why we have the Harrys of the world on the ExCom is beyond me. We're carrying this guy. I put him on a bunch of my files to help him get the hours he needs, and then he goes and bites the hand that feeds him!"

In reality, Dwight knew exactly why Harry was on the ExCom and why he took the stance he did.

Dwight was a member of W&J's informal but important "Red Circle" group. According to legend, at compensation time a previous managing partner had gone through the partnership list and circled in red the lawyers he thought absolutely critical to success. He made sure that in the compensation process the red circles got special attention. The list was never official. In fact, its supposed originator generally denied its existence. However, everybody in the firm knew who was on that list and who was not, and Harry certainly was not.

The Red Circle group was made up of the rainmakers who managed the prestigious clients and brought in new ones. These clients were highly loyal. They saw their W&J partner as a key member of their team whenever an important corporate decision needed to be made. In the early years, it was relatively easy for the Red Circle group to maintain this personal involvement because the firm was small. But as W&J grew spectacularly, largely on the basis of Red Circle accomplishments, the group itself expanded very little.

The Red Circle shouldered the burden of developing and maintaining clients without complaint. They considered it noblesse oblige to make all the critical legal and client-management decisions on the cases. They involved other partners, like Harry, largely to pump up their billable hours, but rarely to collaborate in any meaningful way.

Another aspect of the Red Circle tradition was for members to allow themselves to be under-compensated while over-compensating the dependent partners. This, they thought, promoted a sense of cohesion in the firm.

Dependent partners were allowed on the all-important ExCom to reinforce that same camaraderie, as well as to disguise the existence of the Red Circle.

Not surprisingly, the dependent partners settled into passivity as they watched the Red Circle group perform. They did not strive to take on the challenging responsibilities that would have helped them expand their own capabilities up to leadership caliber. They became ever less involved in the firm's success. And, to be fair, they were not encouraged by the Red Circle partners, who never considered the way in which their own dominant role had marginalized the others.

An additional practice of the dependent partners was to make their own dependence undiscussable and to accept the over-compensation without appearing to acknowledge its existence. Privately, however, they understood their situation and recognized that, unless they were cooperative with the Red Circle group, they risked being cut off from those extra billable hours and the general prosperity of the firm. This feeling of dependence and insulation caused them to resent the Red Circle group, almost in direct proportion to its being the proverbial "hand that feeds." As a result, they tended to band together and to vote as a bloc against any perceived threat to the psychologically demeaning, but economically attractive status quo.

As Dwight saw it, the firm was at a crossroads because of the falling proportion of Red Circle partners in the overall mix. As their proportion fell, the weight on each member to produce and manage greater and greater levels of client billings grew, increasing their antipathy toward the dependent partners. The Red Circle group was eager to make changes because, for the first time, they found themselves unable to take care of the whole firm and preserve its stellar reputation. Staring failure in the face, they came to resent the dependent partners as dead wood.

In response to the impending crisis, the Red Circle group tried to impose an unaccustomed level of discipline on the dependent partners. They instituted a new partner review system, which had as a central tenet that each partner would have to develop his or her own self-sustaining practice. But the vast majority of dependent partners could no more develop a self-sustaining practice than they could fly. During their entire careers they had relied on members of the leadership group not only to provide them with work, but also to guide their efforts on the work by making the critical choices. Harry was a perfect case in point. His cautious pessimism made it impossible for him to attract new clients, who were immediately mortified by his gloomy assessment of their cases. Existing clients were content to have him on their cases, as long as some dynamic (that is, Red Circle) partner was clearly in charge.

The move for this policy shift created widespread misunderstanding and resentment in the firm, heightening the tension already bubbling under the surface. The dependent partners felt that an unfair change had been sprung on them and they were nervous and worried. In large part, the negative reaction resulted from the unilateral nature of the change and the absence of discussion of the underlying rationale. The rationale for the change was obvious—the inability of the Red Circle group to keep carrying the weight. But since its historic role always had been off-limits for discussion, it was difficult now to offer the change as being driven by the breakdown in this tradition.

Despite their fears and concerns, a number of the dependent partners sallied forth into the legal marketplace and tried to play by the new rules. In the main, they developed small-scale, low-margin clients who provided neither the billings nor the prestige generated by those high-profile clients attracted and served by the Red Circle group.

The dependent partners felt awkward and uncomfortable. They resented the arbitrary way in which the long-standing rules of the game had been changed and saw the dawn of a more mean-spirited era for the firm. The Red Circle group saw the dependent partners as lowering historical standards and dragging the firm down toward mediocrity.

At the meeting, Dwight had been responsible for laying out the three or four strategic options for the firm. Given the recent failure and the heightened level of mistrust and misunderstanding, he scrapped all but the mildest of these. Even so, at the ExCom meeting, Harry condemned in almost hysterical terms the consideration of new options so soon after the trauma of the last policy change. Pointing to the stress and consternation many of the other partners were feeling, Harry argued for postponing the consideration of any new initiatives. His position won the day as the ExCom split implicitly along Red Circle and dependent partner lines. Dwight realized that the balance of voting power had shifted, perhaps forever. And as the level of mistrust and misunderstanding increased, the ability to forge consensus on a path forward grew ever more difficult.

At the root of the misunderstanding here is the fact that the initial defining choices of the Red Circle and dependent groups are undiscussable. Without consultation or discussion, the Red Circle group chose to seize more and more responsibility *rather* than work to educate, upgrade the skills of, and integrate the dependent partners. While not evident to the Red Circle partners at the time, an inevitable consequence of their actions was the burden of carrying an increasingly large dependent partner group.

Choice without prior discussion is consistent with the *win, don't lose* governing value. In any discussion about who takes responsibility on client files, the Red Circle partner's view may be challenged and a different result emerge, causing the Red Circle partner's view to lose, or at least not win in entirety. Such a discussion risks the possibility that the Red Circle partner will not *maintain control* because the conversation could head in unexpected directions (for example, by the dependent partner challenging the capabilities of the Red Circle partner). Choice without discussion also serves the desire to *avoid embarrassment* associated with difficult discussions of individual capabilities and to *stay rational* by avoiding an emotional conversation.

The dependent group, of course, also chose the path of passivity rather than work to educate and upgrade their own abilities. While not evident to them at the time, this choice also had problematic long-term consequences.

Of course, choice without discussion also encourages adherence to the governing values for the dependent group. Their views of themselves or others are not publicly challenged and subjected to potential disconfirmation through discussion. The off-limits rule allowed them to avoid conversations that could become heated, potentially out of control, and eventually embarrassing.

Ironically, by not having a conversation about the choices they make, both parties made it likely that the governing values would be strictly maintained. Each group defines winning and maintaining control in ways that suit its respective situation.

It is unclear, and in truth irrelevant, which choice came first: the Red Circle partners' choice or the dependent partners' choice. What is important is that the choices encouraged and reinforced one another, leaving the firm at the mercy of the Responsibility Virus.

Making problematic topics undiscussable is a common defensive practice that psychologist Melanie Klein traced back to the early stages of the mother-child relationship.[1] Elliot Jaques extended her analysis to organizational contexts, showing that the "minimization of anxiety" seems to be a primary objective of many work groups.[2]

In this case, with no explicit discussion, all the partners are left to guess as to what motivated one another's choices. The partners on each side know their own choice well. In addition, each side can observe the actions that define the other side's choices and can think he has a reasonably good understanding of their nature. For example, Harry can observe Dwight attending and leading in all the critical client meetings and excluding him or other professionals from certain key meetings, and he can then draw the inference that Dwight is fully in charge.

However, without discussion, Harry can only guess at Dwight's thought process, at what caused him to seize the lion's share of responsibility and leave little for Harry. And Dwight can only guess why Harry seemed to jump so quickly into the passive role.

Dwight's and Harry's guesses share two qualities. First, as with most guesses in life, they tend to be inaccurate. Despite the considerable time and energy we devote to the practice, even the most discerning, intuitive, empathetic people can achieve, at best, mediocre accuracy in guessing at the reasoning of others.[3] Second, the guessing is biased, once again, to conform to the governing values. Social psychologists have long pointed out that as human minds struggle to make sense of subtle and rapidly changing data, they try to simplify the task by employing stereotypes consistent with the dominant logic of a given social situation.[4]

The Red Circle partners at W&J attribute to the dependent partners the desire to be passive and under-responsible, a guess that they don't seek to confirm before making their decisions on apportioning responsibility. This enables the Red Circle partners to *win, not lose,* by having their agenda for the client or matter in question prevail and by seeing themselves as the leaderly, responsible partners holding up the dependent partners in a heroic fashion. The guess facilitates their ability to *maintain control* by avoiding public discussion of the choice of how to proceed—because they "know" how the dependent partners would want it to work out anyway—and replacing the public discussion with unilateral choice.

Finally, the guess helps the partners *avoid embarrassment* by obviating the need for any public discussion about the apportionment of responsibility and *stay rational* by avoiding a potentially emotional subject. The Red Circle partners argue to themselves that engaging the dependent partners in a discussion of their weaknesses and the need to avoid giving them meaningful responsibility would be terribly embarrassing to those dependent partners. They therefore hold the dependent partners responsible for their unilateral actions, without ever checking whether the dependent partners wanted to avoid such a conversation. Not checking with the dependent partners (and holding them responsible for not checking) produces a secondary useful by-product for the Red Circle partners. They avoid the possibility of a potentially embarrassing conversation in which the dependent partners might dispute, if asked their opinion, the weight of responsibility taken on by the Red Circle partners. Making choices unilaterally therefore helps avoid the embarrassment of being found to be totally wrong.

So it is evident that the Red Circle partners make guesses that are biased toward substantiating the governing values to power the making of choices, choices that are consistent with the governing values of winning, maintaining control, and avoiding embarrassment. However, in doing so they do not raise their level of understanding of the dependent partners, but rather build in their minds a picture of the dependent partners that is untested and largely undiscussable.

Ironically, the dependent partners use the same technique—guessing and unilateral choice—to achieve the same goals—*win, don't lose, maintain control,* and *avoid embarrassment*—in the same silent negotiation. It is a bizarre dance, but in a short-term and limited way, it achieves the desired result.

As the dependent partners see the Red Circle partners start to maneuver, they make a guess about what they are up to and define *win, don't lose* in two respects. First, they accept a restricted and highly doable task at which they are certainly able to succeed. Second, they see themselves as winning by being highly cooperative and supportive, unlike the leadership partners whom they see as acting in a self-centered, imperialistic fashion. The dependent partners, from their own point of view, are engaging in morally upstanding behavior while the Red Circle partners engage in dubious behavior.

The dependent partners seek to *maintain control* by accepting and carefully defining a doable task with which they feel highly comfortable. They frequently go to great lengths to have the task defined precisely and to negotiate the space to do it themselves without any oversight or interference.

The guess about the Red Circle partners' motives helps the dependent partners *avoid embarrassment* by forgoing any public discussion about the apportionment of responsibility. They argue to themselves that engaging the Red Circle partners in a discussion of their insensitive and imperialist behavior pattern would be terribly embarrassing to the Red Circle partners. And such a conversation could become heated enough to threaten their ability to *stay rational.* So, in parallel, they hold the Red Circle partners responsible for their unilateral actions without ever checking whether they wanted to avoid such a conversation.

In mirror fashion, not checking with the Red Circle partners (and holding them responsible for not checking) produces a secondary useful by-product for the dependent partners. They, too, avoid a potentially embarrassing conversation, in which the Red Circle partners might reveal their opinion about the weak capabilities of the dependent partners.

The dependent partners also make guesses that are biased toward substantiating the governing values; they then use these guesses to make choices that are consistent with the governing values of winning, maintaining control, avoiding embarrassment, and staying rational. However, in so doing, they do not raise their level of understanding of the Red Circle partners, but rather build in their minds a picture of the Red Circle partners that is untested and largely undiscussable.

Both sides manage, by their own definitions, to win and to maintain control simultaneously in the same transaction. One might reasonably ask: What is the big problem? Everybody is happy. None of the governing values are violated.

In fact, there is not just one big problem but four. First, the kind of maneuvering I've described sets off the Responsibility Virus. Each party overreacts to the potential for failure, with the Red Circle partners taking on too much responsibility and the dependent partners too little. Static conservation of responsibility pushes them apart to greater and greater levels of over- and under-responsibility. In due course, dynamic conservation takes hold and causes the classic flip to take place, which is evidenced by the advent of the self-sustaining practice policy in which the dependent partners are asked to become over-responsible relative to their capabilities.

The second problem is the rise in misunderstanding. To protect against the possibility of embarrassing conversations and the potential loss of control, both sides guess about—rather than inquire into—the reasoning and motivations of the other party. Inevitably the guesses contain error, especially given the propensity toward bias in service of protecting the governing values. The error creates misunderstanding on the part of each of the two groups about the reasoning and motivations of the other side. And rather than inquire to check whether misunderstanding exists, both sides rigidly avoid inquiring into each other's views, because to do so would risk many forms of embarrassment.

Unchecked misunderstanding deepens. The dependent partners don't understand the reasoning and motivation of the Red Circle partners in taking the first step into over-responsibility. The Red Circle partners don't understand the first step of the dependent partners. However, both sides *think* they *really* understand the other party. And, thanks to the maneuvering described, each party provides the other with data that serve to reinforce the view of the other side. They are even more reinforced when the dependent partners spend what they think is an inordinate amount of time negotiating their exact role and deliverables. The Red Circle partners come to think of the dependent partners as passive, narrow-minded, and bureaucratic—hardly partners at all.

Meanwhile, the dependent partners are reinforced in their view of the Red Circle partners when the latter divide responsibility without so much as a nod in the direction of discussion. They are even more reinforced when the Red Circle partners start to treat them like second-class citizens, becoming abrupt and curt when the dependent partners try to discuss important issues such as deliverables.

Each group's perceptions of the other party influence their treatment of them, which, in turn, causes the other party to act in a fashion consistent with the first party's views, thus reinforcing the views and the treatment. To be consistent with the governing values, the dependent partners act passively, convincing the Red Circle partners they were right in the first place. Hence each party contributes successively to the confirmation of the perceptions of the other party. As a result, each party becomes more convinced of the veracity of their point of view and acts accordingly.

The third problem is that eventually the misunderstanding evolves into mistrust and resentment. Since the parties don't inquire into the reasoning and motivations of one another, they must fill in the blanks by guessing. The guessing often includes attributions of improper or illicit motives, which are never tested. So when actions arise that are not inconsistent with the attributed nasty motives, the motives appear to have been confirmed and mistrust of future motives and actions takes shape. As further misunderstanding leads to exacerbated mistrust, resentment grows.

At W&J, despite the reality that the Red Circle group subsidized the dependent partners to a substantial degree every year for decades, the dependent partners saw the Red Circle group as cruel, capricious, and uncaring; this view was reinforced with the introduction of the self-sustaining practice policy. The dependent partners saw the new policy as an arbitrary and capricious way for the Red Circle group to weed out some of the dependent partners of the firm, and they deeply resented what they saw as an attack on the firm's tradition of teamwork.

Similarly, despite the reality that the dependent partners generally worked very hard to support the Red Circle partners, the Red Circle group saw the dependent partners as lacking initiative and leadership. When the dependent partners reacted negatively to the introduction of the self-sustaining practice policy, the Red Circle partners felt confirmed in their view that they had to continue to carry the ungrateful crowd of complainers.

The truth, of course, is that thanks to the Responsibility Virus both sides contributed mightily to the shortcomings of the other and to the overall atmosphere of mistrust and resentment.

The fourth problem is that the misunderstanding, mistrust, and resentment eventually bring about organizational rigidity. It becomes difficult for any party to propose significant change because such proposals will be greeted with suspicion and mistrust. And the ambient level of mistrust makes it difficult for the concerns about a proposal to be discussed openly. Rather, the true concerns—and their potential resolutions—are typically left buried, only to surface in obscure ways. In this respect, the Responsibility Virus provides a powerful ally for the status quo in organizations.

Mistrust and resentment in the wake of the recent policy failure make it extremely difficult for either group to propose a way out of the dynamic.

CHAPTER 6

Atrophy of
Choice-Making Skills

Ned, a tanned and wiry curmudgeon, is founder, chairman, and principal stockholder of the STG empire. At seventy-one, he still has the energy level of a man half his age. Even though it is well past midnight, he puts in a last call to one of those younger men he often runs circles around, the CEO of his long-distance phone business.

"Just checking in, Dick," Ned begins. "I see the numbers aren't turning around even with the new promotions strategy from the last board meeting."

"Just checking in?" Dick thinks. "This is 'just checking in' the way the Spanish Inquisition was 'just checking in.'"

These late-night interrogations had become standard operating procedure, something friends had warned Dick about when he decided to take the job with STG. Forty-five years old, with a great track record in the communications industry in another country, Dick had picked up his family and relocated for the opportunity to test his wings as a chief executive.

But during the last eighteen months, as Dick settled into the job, Ned had become increasingly overbearing. Early on, the late night calls took the form of questioning decisions . . . was he really sure about it? . . . did he really understand the risks? Later, the calls migrated to suggestions; now they felt more like direct orders, though still posed as questions.

Picturing Ned's leathery scowl at the other end of the line, Dick formulates his goal for this particular call as "don't give him anything to attack, and see what he wants me to do."

"I'm disappointed that the numbers haven't turned around," Dick offers tentatively, "but I'm confident in the new strategy you laid out in the last board meeting."

"That was just a suggestion," Ned shoots back. "You made the decision, Dick, and I hope for your sake it turns out well."

"Good god," Dick mutters to himself. "That was a direct order from the chairman in front of an entire board that voted unanimously, as it always does, for the chairman's proposal. My job wasn't to kick the tires. My job was to follow orders."

Dick responds, "I think it will," but the words come out hollow. He doesn't believe it for a minute.

Ned seems to take Dick's lack of confidence as encouragement to press harder. "Why the hell haven't we really geared up our efforts in the consumer market? All I see is advertising for business customers. We'll never succeed as just a business carrier."

"Ned, you know that's a tough market to penetrate and we need to watch the overheads."

"That's why I hired what I thought was a tough CEO," Ned counters. "I've got bankers coming at me like

panhandlers in pinstripes. But I'm not about to admit defeat just because the going gets a little rough."

"I understand."

"Good, I knew you would. I'll talk to you soon."

The next day Dick gathers his management team and delivers the latest thunderbolt from Ned.

"We're going after the consumer market. Ned sees it as a big priority. I know this is going to be tough, but this is what we're going to do."

Not surprisingly, this pronouncement is greeted with a firestorm of protest. The consumer market is dangerous. This flies in the face of all STG's recent efforts. It makes no strategic sense.

Dick listens silently, and then repeats the word from on high. Citing the authority of the chairman, he tells his team to get on board and come up with their best possible plan.

To no one's surprise, the start-up costs associated with expansion are deadly, and the next quarter results are worse than the quarter before.

At the next board meeting, Ned explodes in rage: "Whose crazy idea was it to pursue the consumer market? We were in dire straits already. Why invite more trouble?"

Dick pales as he listens, too dumbfounded to respond. The "crazy idea" was Ned's! Dick had no choice. What else could he have done but implement the plan the chairman demanded?

At the end of the board meeting, Ned convenes an executive committee session that excludes management. He wants to let the board know that the banks are pressuring him to give up control of the long-distance business to keep from going under. But in the meantime, as far as Ned is concerned, Dick is on the way out. The chairman is engaging an executive search firm to find a new CEO.

Choice-Making Capability

In choice-making ability as in any other skill, performance levels rarely remain static. We either get better or we get worse, and to get better we need to set goals. In meta-analytical studies of motivation, the setting of goals was one of the most successful of all possible interventions.[1] When we set goals, we take ownership of—responsibility for—a particular behavior. We come to own both the pitfalls and the benefits of producing that behavior, which in turn becomes an extension of our own identity.

The key, however, is the setting of goals that are realistic but that nevertheless stretch our capabilities, placing us in a zone where we are neither anxious about failing nor bored with a task that's become routine. This is the zone that researchers such as Mihaly Csikszentmihalyi have labeled "peak performance."[2]

If I've never played tennis before, the first step I must take if I want to learn is to try to simply hit the ball back and forth across the net. I must take responsibility for a task that exceeds my current capability . . . but by only a small measure. If as a first step I bite off too much—trying to master a perfect serve, for instance—I'll be overwhelmed. I'll get frustrated and probably quit, because I took on too great a stretch in responsibility.

The best way for me to grow as a tennis player is to go to a teaching pro who will work with me on the proper grip and stance and start me out hitting easy shots. The pro will nurse me along by giving me a succession of tasks that stretch my existing capability level but don't break it. As I execute each stretching task, my capability will grow incrementally. In this way, establishing responsibility slightly above capability provides a constant upward tug on capability.

FIGURE 6.1   Productive Development of Capabilities

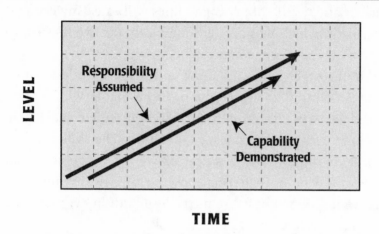

TIME

But let's imagine that I return for my sixth lesson with my teaching pro but he's out sick. The manager of the tennis club assigns me another professional who thinks I've come for my second lesson. If I passively go along with his regimen—still hitting those easy shots back and forth across the net—I will probably progress little, if at all, because he will have me taking on responsibility for tasks that were stretching four lessons ago, but are far too easy now. I would return for my seventh lesson no better off than when I came for my sixth lesson. At that point, I would suffer only an opportunity cost. That is, I would have forgone the opportunity to improve during the course of my sixth lesson, and stagnated instead.

However, if in some bizarre time warp, like Bill Murray in *Groundhog Day*, I keep showing up for what the professional treats as my second lesson, my skills will gradually atrophy. My stroke will regress to approximately where it was after my actual second lesson, because I am not practicing anything I learned during lessons three through five. The absence of any testing of my capabilities will cause my capability growth, which was accelerating nicely for five lessons, to stop and then reverse course.

On the other hand, if I show up for my sixth lesson in a cocky mood and challenge the pro to a match with $1,000 on the line, I won't grow my capabilities either. He'll mop the court with me and pocket my money. The skill required to beat the pro would be so far above my capabilities that there would be no beneficial upward tug. If anything, the massive failure might cause me to lose faith in ever learning the game and force me to take up golf.

In both under-responsibility and over-responsibility there is a substantial mismatch between capability demonstrated and responsibility assumed.

As responsibility swings from one side to the other, we spend most of our time and effort *either* working below *or* significantly above the level of our capabilities, either coasting along too easily or failing miserably. Only for a tiny proportion of time are we in a capabilities-enhancing mode. That zone of peak performance exists only when we have assumed a slight over-responsibility, which, as we master the task, becomes an under-responsibility. Then it's time to take on a new, more challenging task, which repeats the cycle again.

Constant challenge is the only way to maintain the consistent upward tug that comes from assuming responsibilities above our current capabilities. Without this beneficial tug, growth stops and atrophy sets in.

On the tennis court, playing to your existing ability will bring your game down and your skills will regress. The same is true of your choice-making responsibility on the job.

FIGURE 6.2 Atrophy of Capabilities

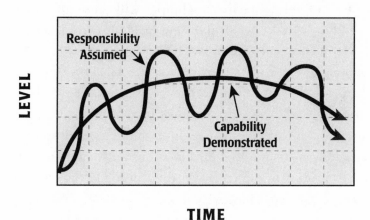

TIME

Capability Diminution at STG

Dick came to STG with much success under his belt but ready for an entrepreneurial experience to expand his skills. In bowing to Ned's overbearing leadership, he did not take on growth responsibilities. Instead, he slowly retreated from the task of making the critical decisions he was hired to make, and he was reduced to passively carrying out the chairman's bidding. Not only did Dick lower his responsibility level, his management team did as well. Unbeknownst to Dick, they had begun lowering their collective responsibility level two deposed CEOs earlier.

In due course, Dick was making choices at a level not just below what he was hired to do, but at a level below that at which he had operated at his previous job. He was now operating more like a COO than a CEO. This, in turn, put downward pressure on his COO, who adjusted his own choice-making accordingly. In eighteen months on the job, Dick never advanced his capability as a top decisionmaker. Had a disappointed Ned not fired him, his basic managerial capabilities would have begun to atrophy.

Meanwhile, Ned swirled ever higher into over-responsibility, attempting to make all the key choices across all his companies. Brilliant, tough, and experienced as he was, not even Ned could stay on top of the intimate details of four firms in four rapidly evolving and highly competitive businesses. His ability to make good decisions in the long-distance business was dubious at best. But having prompted Dick to slide into under-responsibility, he was forced to fill Dick's vacuum.

The negative fallout went well beyond having to sell off control of the long-distance business to appease the banks. In the other businesses, there was increased pressure on Ned to let them manage instead of having to constantly react to his whims. Rather than being seen as a wise, old baron whose capabilities were still getting stronger, Ned was increasingly seen as an intrusive owner whose time had passed and whose usefulness had faded.

Capability Diminution
in the Previous Cases

At *Wapshot*, saving the computer account by herself was beyond Caroline's existing capability. True, her sub-optimal choices led to initial failure. But had Michael reacted to the failure in a balanced manner by offering to collaborate and provide advice on how Caroline could overcome her challenges, she might well have learned an important lesson from the failure and built her choice-making capabilities for the next time. Instead, Michael assumed total responsibility. He made all the critical choices, and Caroline assumed a role well below her capabilities, a role Michael signaled as proper for her going forward. As she slid into that role, she began the process of capability atrophy.

Michael had the opportunity to take on a challenge—mentoring a senior executive—that was probably the appropriate sort of stretch for him as a leader and manager. Instead he slid back into the role of super-salesman, a role so comfortable for him that it provided no particular challenge. He could make a sales director's key choices on autopilot. But in doing so, he implicitly abdicated responsibility for broad leadership of the magazine, the publisher's role that would have challenged him and forced him to grow. In due course, the time commitment associated with the easy super-salesman role crowded out the time required to consider and make the key choices associated with running a magazine. The magazine languished, and Michael failed.

At GPC, the coping mechanism of narrow perfectionism led not just to diminished capability building, but also to capability atrophy. Managers delegated complexity downward, narrowing their decisionmaking responsibility, defining victory narrowly, and avoiding risk. They didn't build their skills in complex problem solving or in breakthrough thinking or in creating out-of-the-box choices. By avoiding risk, they never learned the art of prudently taking on risk. And by focusing on inspecting and selling, they didn't learn how to work collaboratively.

At GPC, the seeking of narrow perfectionism eventually caused the choice-making skills of managers to atrophy. By narrowing the scope and importance of the choices they needed to make, they failed to practice and enhance their choice-making skills. These skills slowly withered away as each manager worked on his or her own little set of doable tasks.

No matter how much Jerry wished for stretching and aggressiveness, the managers were unwilling to rise to a challenge they were no longer capable of meeting.

Lack of capability enhancement reinforces the fear of failure. Managers are faced with ever more complex and difficult choices as they rise through their organizations. Often they get promoted because they prove successful at creating coping mechanisms. Yet as they rise, the complexity they face increases. This magnifies their fear of failure, which in time overwhelms their ability to cope.

At the IDA, the Cameroonian project had the potential to be a great learning opportunity for Pierre. While he had great technical and analytical capabilities in development economics, he had underdeveloped "soft" skills—that is, the ability to collaborate productively to make change happen. Ironically, he needed help from the last place he was inclined to look—the Cameroonians. He needed their help to build his understanding of the interpersonal side of economic development. He needed their help in teaching him how to collaborate more effectively.

However, Pierre signaled from the inception his intention to be totally in charge of all choice-making on the project. In failing spectacularly and independently, Pierre learned almost nothing in the areas in which his capabilities needed the most improvement.

Likewise, the Cameroonian players learned little or nothing from this project, thanks to their passive under-responsible stance. Pierre had much to offer based on his development experience in many countries. Had they collaborated closely and shared the choice-making responsibilities with Pierre, the Cameroonians could have learned a great deal and advanced their own skills. Instead they simply experienced a failure from which there were few, if any, useful takeaways.

At DevTek the diminution of capability was not quite as evident. In this case, what was more obvious was the absence of growth in a key skill, the skill of collaboration per se.

At the law firm W&J, the atrophy of capabilities was highly evident. The dependent partners, like Harry, fell easily into comfortable roles in which they stopped challenging themselves and, as a result, stopped growing. Over time, these bright graduates of the top law schools became less and less familiar with the latest legal trends and less capable of independent choice-making. Not only did their choice-making skills stop growing, but the *courage* needed to make choices withered as well.

By choosing their over-responsible path, the Red Circle partners learned virtually nothing about assisting young lawyers to grow into leadership, which became the greatest failing of the firm. They never learned to balance the need for garnering new work themselves with nurturing the client management skills of bright young partners.

The atrophy of skills can be seen widely in the global economy as a whole. Perhaps the most famous and obvious example was IBM's slow, painful descent leading up to its crash in 1992–1993. Through the 1950s, 1960s, and 1970s, the decades of the firm's most rapid expansion, IBM's leadership explicitly promised its entire workforce lifetime employment. The guarantee was seen as critical to success because it was such an attractive inducement in recruiting. However, it created an environment in which leadership assumed all the responsibility. There was no felt need for all employees to collaborate with leadership to keep the comp.. ıy competitive. No one felt the need to hone job skills to maintain their value to IBM or, should the need arise, to find a job elsewhere.

As we know, this environment of under-responsibility in the workforce and paternalistic over-responsibility in leadership produced a complacent culture that was blown off the road as the computer market fragmented and competition intensified in the late 1980s. In 1992, the promise of limitless job security was broken. Big Blue stunned the world by announcing an $8.5 billion write-off, followed by an $11.6 billion write-off in 1993, to cover the cost of cutting more than 100,000 employees. Many IBM lifers, ill-equipped for the fierce competition coming from Silicon Valley, Austin, and Research Triangle Park, felt horrified and betrayed. In addition, they were no longer in high demand, as they had been in earlier times when IBM on your resume meant a guaranteed attractive exit with one call to a headhunter. Why? It was obvious to outsiders that the once-vaunted skills had atrophied.

Similarly, McDonald's Restaurants during its period of expansion and domination of the U.S., then global, fast-food business provided what was seen as a "covenant" to its franchisees. The deal was: Invest $250,000 to $500,000 in building a restaurant and work in that restaurant for the next five to ten years and you will be rich. McDonald's implied that success was certain, but as with IBM leadership, this was not something that McDonald's could ensure. Fierce competition, market saturation, and McDonald's complacency ensured instead that the covenant would be broken by the mid-1990s. Angry franchisees complained vociferously to leadership, but had acquired little in the way of skills to reverse the decline in the value of their businesses.

Overseas, the Japanese lifetime employment system, long lauded by many in the West for its progressiveness, has contributed to the inability of Japan to turn around its moribund economy as its major corporations struggle against entrenched labor practices and a labor force that can't or won't help.

An even more insidious side effect of the Responsibility Virus is the way in which we lose touch with how we would have felt, and what we would have been capable of accomplishing, had our skills continued to build in optimal fashion.

At *Wapshot*, Caroline lost touch with her sense of her potential. She felt only a vague sense of unease at her lack of forward momentum. At the same time, Michael lost confidence in his skills above the level of the super-salesman role which he mastered long before. Managers at GPC enjoyed the feeling of perfectionism, but wondered why the business wasn't prospering. They lost touch with what it feels like to be stretched and what it means to dig deep to discover their fullest capabilities.

After the fading away of both Pierre and his project, the Cameroonian officials got together to begin work on a project of their own and found themselves pulling out Pierre's plan. Because they were so angry with him for abandoning them, they focused on that emotion, not on the disquiet arising from their inability to come up with anything good on their own. Trouble is, with the likes of Pierre and the IDA around, they have, until now, never forced themselves to think hard about their own development.

At DevTek, the executives wondered why they found global competition so difficult and why they seemed to be outflanked by their competitors. Dependent partners at W&J set out to create a self-sustaining practice and wondered why it seemed so difficult. And at STG, Dick wondered why this job as CEO seemed so above his head when he was such a star performer in the last one.

Never achieving, and not knowing—this is the greatest price paid by victims of the Responsibility Virus.

PART 3

Tools for Inoculating
Against the Virus

CHAPTER 7

The Choice
Structuring Process

Once the biggest bank in its market, First Bank of Commerce had been overtaken in several key areas by smaller competitors. A number of these smaller, more agile competitors had chosen specific lines of business on which to concentrate and dominate. Meanwhile, FBC had continued to try to compete everywhere, still acting like the grand institution it once was. In the past decade FBC had made very few strategic choices other than to keep on doing what it was doing.

Not surprisingly, this lack of decisiveness and initiative had produced two problems. First, Wall Street analysts had come to see FBC as a slow-moving dinosaur. Second, investors had learned to love FBC's more narrowly targeted competitors. Several firms FBC had once considered buying now had stock market caps high enough to buy FBC . . . with ease.

FBC had been an autocratic institution for more than fifty years. CEOs had always retreated to their executive offices and made decisions that were to be carried out dutifully by the organization, but in the past decade, this system had worked less and less effectively. The industry had become far more complicated and begun changing at a pace never seen before. Rather than retreating to his office to make decisions, the previous CEO retreated to his office to avoid decisions.

In the face of this inertia and drift, Horst, a thirty-five-year veteran of the bank, had come to the helm. He knew FBC and everybody in it well, but the market had hung an albatross around his neck, calling him the "safe inside choice," bound up in the internal culture and the mindset that had produced the current problems. And he had to admit that he looked the part, from his conservative dress to his thinning silver hair to his slow, deliberate speaking style.

But Horst knew the bank needed a strategy and it needed one in a hurry. The crew was demoralized. Shareholders were ready to jump ship. Even the regulators were expressing concerns about the long-term viability of the bank. According to FBC tradition, he should go off, think deeply, and come back with a strategy, but he knew that this wouldn't work. He didn't have all the answers. He needed the help of his senior managers to make choices, and he needed them to be fully committed emotionally to those choices.

Going against the bank's history and culture, he drew together some of his most trusted senior managers to create a strategy collaboratively. The group included: Mitch, the head of retail banking; James, the head of corporate banking; Pamela, the head of corporate strategy; Neil, the head of credit cards; and Wally, the head of the emerging electronic banking business.

The group and its mandate represented a challenge from the beginning. First, everyone assumed that the exercise was largely a charade, and that Horst would eventually make the strategy decisions himself, especially if his thinking diverged from the group's. Second, most of the group members saw themselves as vying for Horst's job and therefore felt more competitive with one another than collaborative. Third, they really didn't trust each other. There had been flare-ups between several of them and their views of the future of the banking business differed substantially.

For Horst, however, the die was cast. He was going to pursue a strategy collaboratively whether his team believed him or not.

The Problems with Group Choice-Making

Horst faced a classic Responsibility Virus infection. At FBC, the governing values had already undermined effective collaboration. In keeping with the *win, don't lose* injunction, his colleagues didn't really want to listen to one another, lest they become convinced their own point of view is wrong, which would be seen as a loss.

To *maintain control*, they didn't want to engage in open-ended brainstorming that might lead in unanticipated, and uncomfortable, directions. And finally, to *avoid embarrassment* and *stay rational* they might prefer not to reveal any point of view and the logic behind it, for fear of being criticized in a way that made them feel belittled and perhaps angry.

Bob Abelson, a psychologist, has described the human tendency to treat our beliefs as if they were possessions as we struggle to maintain the illusions of "victory," "control," and "dignity."[1] Those "possessions" often include a rich personal mythology, divorced from observations and others' criticisms, that we fear will be put at risk if we engage in truly collaborative behavior. As a result of this defensive posturing, groups rarely bring to decisionmaking any more firepower than that provided by a single individual.

That's how groups like Horst's risk one or more of four negative outcomes of group decisionmaking:

1. No consensus. The group never engages the problem sufficiently to reach a choice. It simply postpones making a decision and suffers whatever costs accompany delay—a well-established tradition at places like FBC.

2. Bad consensus. The group reaches a poor decision because it does not make full use of the logic and data from all members to make a robust choice. Instead, the Responsibility Virus causes the logic and data of the over-responsible member to be weighed solely or at very least too heavily, and the logic and data of the under-responsible members to be ignored or suppressed as these members retreat and watch. This is commonly known as "groupthink."[2] It is a mechanism of selective collusion around sub-optimal commitments, which psychologists have long described in terms of conformity pressures, fear of conflict, and anxiety caused by the fear of abandonment.[3]

3. False consensus. The group appears to reach a choice, when in fact under-responsible members simply have not voiced their opposition. In such situations, the silent parties typically drag their feet in taking action on the choice, subsequently undermine the choice, or ask at a future point that the choice be revisited. As Paul Nickerson has pointed out, we maintain many

theories about what others think—and even about what they think we think—that are often false.[4] In other words, we kid ourselves, choosing to believe whatever serves our purposes.

4. Weak consensus. The parties eke out a consensus for which there is minimal enthusiasm and commitment. Such choices typically get unwound or reversed at the first sign of trouble. A weak consensus is the path of least resistance, the next best thing to making no decision, often prompted by a directive coming from on high to make a decision quickly.

The Requirements of a Group Choice-Making Process

The challenge for Horst at FBC, and for all leaders, is to find a choice-making process for groups that:

- Produces robust and compelling choices, and
- Does so without violating the governing values, thus triggering the Responsibility Virus.

Robust and compelling choices come from sound logic applied to valid and representative data. The only way we can be sure we have sound logic and valid data is if both are subjected to thorough and open testing. We can only be sure that we have representative data if we draw it from all relevant group members.

But once again, testing is inherently frightening because it threatens to violate *win, don't lose*. A representative selection of data is hard to achieve when members withhold it to avoid subjecting it to the frightening prospect of testing. And each person brings his or her own personal, idiosyncratic baggage to the conversation, challenging enough for others to comprehend, let alone deal with. That's why an environment of safety and encouragement is essential for a successful group choice process.

To provide an environment in which the group members feel comfortable supplying their data and reasoning, we first need to understand how they form their opinions.

How We Reason

Each member of a group will have data from his or her experiences, data that is applicable in some way to the choice at hand, and a personal logic structure for considering the choice. Left to their own devices, the members may draw from the pool of data available to them—results, past experiences, and so on—and add to the data any number of layers of reasoning or inference to reach a conclusion.

Let's say that Sandy, a VP at VisionTech, an innovative manufacturer of office products for business customers, goes out to interview an existing customer, and in doing so gathers data in the form of a customer's opinion. However, because she's human, she doesn't remember everything she hears. Instead, she selects some data to register loud and clear and other data to ignore.

Sandy selects as truly important the first half of the customer's statement—"I really like VisionTech. It has been an innovative leader in this business for a long time." What fails to register with her is the latter half—"But I'm coming under increasing cost pressure and have to make tradeoffs."

She then tries to make sense of the data by applying successive layers of logic to it, first paraphrasing it in order to store it (creating a "sound-bite"), then naming it (as we'd

FIGURE 7.1   The Ladder of Inference

Sandy decides what to do
(Innovation and leadership are the most critical avenues to pursue)

Sandy understands / evaluates what is happening
(Customers will stick with us if we continue to innovate and lead)

Sandy names the data
(Customers value leadership and innovation)

Sandy paraphrases the data
(This customer values our leadership and innovation)

Sandy selects the data
(I really like VisionTech. It has been an innovative leader for a long time)

Customer   I really like VisionTech. It has been an innovative leader in this business for a long time. But I'm coming under increasing pressure and have to make tradeoffs.

name a computer file), then evaluating it as to consequences, and finally arriving at a choice of action.

In her choice-making, Sandy is climbing something Chris Argyris terms the Ladder of Inference.[5] As she moves upward, the inferences applied remove Sandy further and further from the initial data. Anybody other than Sandy would have a difficult time intuiting the specific reasoning steps that take her from the data to the conclusion. Also, as she climbs, whatever errors may have occurred in her initial data selection become magnified many times over.

The only way to overcome problems such as flawed or incomplete data is by making the data and the logical inferences explicit, and then subjecting them to testing by the other members of the group. By vetting the data and logic in an open and challenging discussion, the Ladder of Inference is validated and a robust choice can result.

But the choice also must be *compelling*; that is, it must generate group commitment to take actions based on the choice. To generate this kind of commitment, each group member must feel that the group properly weighed his or her individual contribution of data and logic. This represents a challenge for the choice process in two respects.

The first challenge arises because fundamental disagreements can occur anytime each member of the group applies his or her own pattern of reasoning to their own accumulated data. In other words, individual group members can look at the same body of evidence and reach conclusions that are highly contradictory. They develop "Dueling Ladders of Inference."[6]

Sandy and Richard, another VisionTech VP who was at the same meeting, pick up on different pieces of the customer's message. The difference is as simple as paying attention to the first half versus paying attention to the second. However, as each manager adds reasoning to the incomplete and conflicting data, the differences multiply, and Sandy and Richard reach conclusions that are irreconcilable. At that high level of inference, neither manager can understand how the other got to his or her conclusion. Standing at the top of

FIGURE 7.2 Dueling Ladders

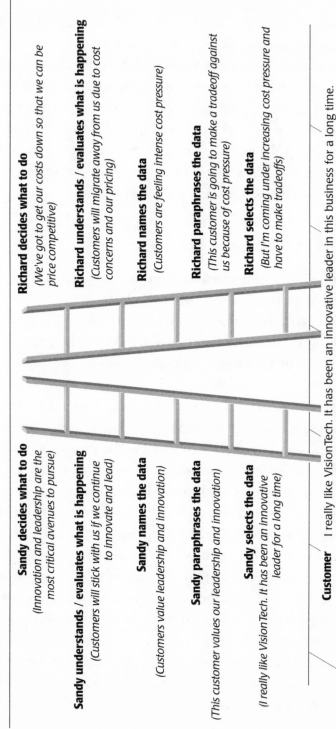

Sandy decides what to do
(Innovation and leadership are the most critical avenues to pursue)

Sandy understands / evaluates what is happening
(Customers will stick with us if we continue to innovate and lead)

Sandy names the data
(Customers value leadership and innovation)

Sandy paraphrases the data
(This customer values our leadership and innovation)

Sandy selects the data
(I really like VisionTech. It has been an innovative leader for a long time.)

Richard decides what to do
(We've got to get our costs down so that we can be price competitive)

Richard understands / evaluates what is happening
(Customers will migrate away from us due to cost concerns and our pricing)

Richard names the data
(Customers are feeling intense cost pressure)

Richard paraphrases the data
(This customer is going to make a tradeoff against us because of cost pressure)

Richard selects the data
(But I'm coming under increasing cost pressure and have to make tradeoffs)

Customer   I really like VisionTech. It has been an innovative leader in this business for a long time. But I'm coming under increasing pressure and have to make tradeoffs.

their separate ladders, each begins shouting that the other "simply doesn't get it."

To be compelling for Sandy and Richard, any choice must bridge the chasm between their very distinct conclusions.

But as we've seen before, fear, and the Virus it spreads, make it very difficult for group members to make explicit what drives them to their conclusions. The governing values push them to withdraw rather than risk an embarrassing or defeating challenge to their data and logic.

Key Design Features of a Group Process

Ridding our conference rooms of the Responsibility Virus requires steps that address the governing values.

To avoid violating the value of *win, don't lose,* the process must disassociate options from individuals. Options must be owned by the group. If an option falls by the wayside as it is processed and considered, it is the group's option, not a single individual's. This is particularly important for those individuals who are particularly sensitive to not being seen to be losing by others in a group. The process should also avoid creating points of tension where conflicting opinions seek to prevail over each other. Rather, conflicting positions should be resolved based on the assembling of new data, which the conflicting parties can then see as legitimate.

To avoid violating the value of *maintain control,* all individuals must feel that they can meaningfully influence any aspect of interest to them, whenever they feel the need. If they have particular interest in a given option, they must feel that they alter the manner in which that option is considered. If they are skeptical about a given option, they must be given the right to set the test for the option and the standard of proof for the test. They must never feel that they have no recourse during the process but to either grab the reins or withdraw. This is particularly critical for the individuals whose pattern is to withdraw when they feel that they are losing control of a situation.

To avoid violating the value of *avoid embarrassment,* the process must once again disassociate options from individuals. Group members should not fear that by introducing an option, they will have that option forever hung around their neck, then dismissed in a manner that causes embarrassment. Again, some individuals are hyper-sensitive to the feeling of embarrassment because they feel intellectually inferior to others in the group. For this reason, the process also must seek complete, even extreme inclusiveness. The group must draw out every option, no matter how outlandish. That way no one will be viewed as pushing his own radical agenda, only to have such options dismissed as too extreme. This also ensures that group members can *stay rational* because there is a logical, not emotional, reason for including every option.

Overall, the group process must inoculate against the downsides of the governing values, including the extreme manifestations that are present due to the specific personal baggage group members bring to the table.

The Choice Structuring Process

When Horst first asked for my help in creating a new strategy for FBC, I used a tool I'd created called the Choice Structuring Process.

Horst used the opportunity of an initial choice-setting meeting to reinforce the message that he did not intend to make the choice himself, but rather to make the choice as a group. Many group members did not fully believe him, but

FIGURE 7.3   The Choice Structuring Process

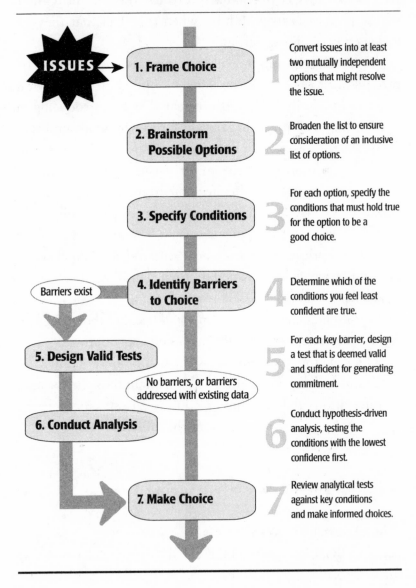

ISSUES ➔

1. Frame Choice

Convert issues into at least two mutually independent options that might resolve the issue.

2. Brainstorm Possible Options

Broaden the list to ensure consideration of an inclusive list of options.

3. Specify Conditions

For each option, specify the conditions that must hold true for the option to be a good choice.

Barriers exist

4. Identify Barriers to Choice

Determine which of the conditions you feel least confident are true.

5. Design Valid Tests

For each key barrier, design a test that is deemed valid and sufficient for generating commitment.

No barriers, or barriers addressed with existing data

6. Conduct Analysis

Conduct hypothesis-driven analysis, testing the conditions with the lowest confidence first.

7. Make Choice

Review analytical tests against key conditions and make informed choices.

the initial signal helped them choose not to retreat into an under-responsible stance. Then we worked our way through the seven steps.

1) Frame Choice

As a general rule, until a choice is framed *as a choice*—as a point at which an irreversible commitment is converged upon—it cannot be made. Furthermore, until a choice is framed as a choice, the group members will not truly engage in the process, because they cannot yet understand the consequences of the choice.

The group must look beyond the problem or issue at hand to discern the type of tradeoff the problem embodies and the type of choice the problem requires. Until a minimum of two mutually exclusive options are identified that would neutralize the issue or problem, the choice is not framed.

A fundamental commitment to openness of the group process (otherwise it is not a group process) requires that, if any member of the group feels that a given option is important, then it should be included in the choice set. Culling an option about which a particular individual feels strongly not only invites embarrassment, in violation of the governing principle, but it will probably cause that individual to withdraw into an under-responsible stance—in such cases, often called a sulk—perhaps for the rest of the process.

However, somebody else in the group may take umbrage at a choice's being explicitly considered. Perhaps they consider the choice dangerous. They may feel that the process will get out of control with such a choice on the table. Concerns of this sort must be taken seriously; otherwise the process violates the governing value of maintaining control. A person with this complaint must be assured that if at any point the discussion of that choice appears to start veering out of control, it will be brought back into control using the process.

At FBC, the group concluded that the critical choice was whether to stay broadly based and make the breadth really work to FBC's advantage, or to pare businesses to focus on a narrower range and utilize the focus to win decisively in those arenas. Identifying this choice helped the group engage, because everyone understood the consequences of the choice. Each executive now knew that, depending on the outcome of the deliberation, the business they were running might be sold off.

This was an especially important issue for Neil, the head of the credit card business. Neil had always been miffed because whenever narrowing the portfolio was discussed, the example used was credit cards. Neil believed that this reflex happened because credit cards would be the easiest to divest, not necessarily the wisest. And as a bit of a scrapper who had worked his way up the industry by working in the least sexy businesses, he always feared that he was treated as a second-class citizen by his executive peers.

But by listening to the group discuss a number of ways FBC could narrow its portfolio, Neil became convinced that the group was willing to engage the tougher choices. They weren't just looking for the easy answer, or to dismiss him or his business.

---

2) Brainstorm Possible Options

Framing the issue as a choice identifies a subset of options, but the next task is to broaden the list.

The objective in this step is to be inclusive rather than restrictive of the number and diversity of options on the table. Later in the process the team will refine and prune the list. Again, it is important to create an atmosphere in which options can be put on the table without fear of embarrassment. Options should be welcomed, not carefully vetted for inclusion. Certainly they should never be trivialized or dismissed. The later steps of the Choice Structuring Process will weed out options that are not viable.

An option should be thought of as a narrative or scenario, a happy story that describes a positive outcome. The story should have internal consistency in its logic, but does not need to be proven at this point. In fact, no one need even assert that it is valid. As long as we can imagine that it *could* be valid, it has made the cut until later, when the time comes for testing. Characterizing the options as stories helps ensure that they are not seen negatively as *your opinion, biased,* or *unsubstantiated.* They are simply ways of thinking that may or may not be proven to have validity. This characterization helps meet the goal of inclusiveness, ensuring that more radical, out-of-the-box ideas are put on the table. There is plenty of time for the process to reduce the option set, but the process will underachieve if the range of options is limited at the front end.

Characterizing options as stories also helps group members discuss the possibilities. People think most easily in stories. It is much easier for someone to tell me a story about why this option could well make sense, rather than give me the data and logic that support this option.

In this step it is critical to create a climate that discourages passive, under-responsible behavior by welcoming options enthusiastically. It is also important to discourage over-responsible behavior, helping the most likely perpetrators recognize that the whole group is engaged and they do not have to take charge.

At their first meeting, the FBC group came up with six options. At their second meeting, they added three more for a total of nine. Toward the end of the second meeting, they marveled collectively that they had come up with and were going to consider such radical ideas. One option was the status quo. Another contemplated maintaining the current broad portfolio but seeking to leverage it for competitive advantage. However, six options entailed dramatically narrowing the portfolio by selling off existing businesses and buying new ones. Under any of these six options, the bank would be radically transformed. The final option, raised by Horst, was the "exit option" in which FBC would put itself on the block. Several members of the group were staggered that Horst had introduced this possibility, thinking that he would consider it out of the question.

The group also expressed surprise that exiting the credit card business and the corporate business made the list without the vigorous opposition of the heads of those respective divisions. But the spirit of inclusiveness and thoroughness trumped such parochial and turf-protecting concerns.

---

3) Specify Conditions

Before an option can make the cut as something to which the group could commit themselves, they must specify the conditions that would need to be substantiated in order to believe that the story is sound.

To identify these key conditions, I use a process I call "reverse-engineering," filling in the Ladder of Inference for each option. Starting from an assumption that the conclusion is valid, we want to fill in the logic and data that would have to hold true. At this stage of the process, we are still not interested in any group member's opinions as to *whether* the conditions pertaining to a given option *are* true. We just want to know *what would have to be true* for every member of the group to feel committed.

This third step in the process invites those in the group with reservations about a particular option to speak out. Making the origins of these reservations clear will enable each possibility to be tested in public, rather than tested privately in the minds of group members. If the conditions survive the test, the public validation will generate commitment to action. If conditions are invalidated, then the generator of the option will see that the option has been fairly considered and failed on its merits.

The process continues to tack away from win/lose and emotionally charged situations. Every member's conditions are given equal consideration to ensure that there is no reluctance caused by fear of embarrassment. Options are reverse-engineered by the group, not the individual who raised the option. Nobody is allowed to voice opinions as to conditions that they believe do not hold true, in order to stay away from unhelpful win/lose dynamics.

At the end of reverse-engineering, each group member understands the logic of each option and the conditions that would have to hold for all members of the group.

The FBC group reverse-engineered the nine options and, despite the radical possibilities embedded in the options, remained calm and friendly throughout.

Though this step was not supposed to evaluate options, the group looked at the conditions for two of the options and felt, to a person, that these conditions were so implausible that they should be dropped from the list. This would not be surprising except for the fact that one of the two options eliminated was the status quo. That is to say, the group felt that the conditions necessary for the status quo to prevail were so implausible that the option needed no further consideration. That meant an end to the bank's strategy, as they knew it. Each member of the group was committed to change.

4) Identify Barriers to Choice

The fourth step in the Choice Structuring Process executes a 180-degree flip. In the previous step, we stayed far, far away from opinions as to whether or not conditions held true, and rather asked the abstract question: What conditions would have to hold true? Now we want to know what conditions each member of the group feels *are least likely to hold true.* These conditions define the barrier to the group's finding the option in question to be compelling. The status quo will prevail over any option until such time as each of these barriers is overcome.

In this step it is extremely important to pay close attention to the member of the group who is most skeptical that a condition actually holds true, because he or she will represent the greatest impediment to the selection and pursuit of that option. For example, a condition for the (mythical) "Expand the Product Line" option is that customers prefer a broader product line to greater product-performance features. The VP of sales, based on his years of experience with customers, is skeptical. In fact, he believes the opposite to be true. The VP of sales will overtly or covertly work to prevent or undermine the "Expand the Product Line" option until such time that he is able to convince himself that customers actually do prefer a broader product line to greater performance features.

Skeptical group members must be encouraged to raise, not suppress, concerns. It doesn't matter why the person is concerned, just that he or she is concerned. And once a concern is raised, the group must take such issues seriously. If the concern is ridiculed or dismissed, other potential problems will be unilaterally suppressed as the individuals with doubts slide into an under-responsible stance, not wishing to face such public embarrassment. If the group does not take up a member's concern as a group, the individual raising the concern will feel singularly responsible for addressing it, which is equally problematic.

If the key skepticisms of the members are drawn out and taken seriously, it helps each member feel that he or she is maintaining control. They won't worry overly much that an option they feel is nonsensical will be approved, because they are able to ensure that their conditions are taken seriously. By the same token, they needn't worry about their favorite option being dismissed. Only analytical testing, which they will help design, or agreement of every member of the group can remove an option from consideration.

In addition, if the options, conditions, and barriers are treated as products of the group rather than an appendage of specific individuals, then the fears generated by the threat of losing and of suffering embarrassment are significantly reduced. All of the above reduces the likelihood that any group member will become passive, or, conversely, try to seize control.

At FBC, Horst's group identified and prioritized the barrier conditions for each of the seven remaining options. Since

the concerns of all parties were being taken into account
with respect to each option, no one felt the singular responsibility to defend a given option against the concerted
opposition, even when that option would have a very direct
impact on his or her own bailiwick.

After reflecting on the conditions and barriers, the
group found itself united in its feeling that two more options were fundamentally infeasible. One of the dismissed
options would have made Neil's business the centerpiece
of the whole strategy, and various members had from the
beginning harbored concerns about Neil's objectivity. So
to the rest of the group, Neil's concurrence on the dis-
missal of this option was a pleasant surprise. After this
meeting to define barriers, several group members were
shaking their heads, wondering where they had picked up
their obviously flawed impression of Neil's partisanship
and inflexibility.

5) Design Valid Tests

Once key barrier conditions are identified, they must be
tested in ways the entire group will find compelling. The test
may involve surveying a thousand customers or speaking to
only one supplier. The test may entail crunching thousands
of numbers or avoiding any. The critical issue is whether the
decisionmaking group regards the test as valid.

The most skeptical member of the group is the most critical for test design. Typically, he or she will have the highest
standard of proof for the test, and building his or her commitment to the choice will be the most challenging. However,
without his or her commitment, the "consensus" will inevitably be false.

The ultimate goal is to design tests that will enable each member of the group to put hand on heart and commit both to making a choice and to taking action on the choice if the analysis confirms the condition.

Group members may have quite different and incompatible tests that they view as valid, resulting in the need to apply multiple tests for a given condition. However, in practice, groups tend to find themselves coalescing around a single acid test, especially if they take their cue from the most skeptical member of the group.

The FBC group was mortified when I told them of my intent to allow the group's most skeptical member to set the standard of proof and to lead in the design of the test in question. They voiced a heartfelt concern that this would lead to the setting of stratospherically high standards of proof that could never be met, thereby providing an implicit veto over options by skeptical members.

I asked the group to give it a try and, to their amazement, not one member set a test or a standard of proof that the group considered excessive. By the time test design rolled around, the group members were comfortable that they were not going to get out of control, they wouldn't be embarrassed, and they were not trapped in a win-or-lose situation. As a result, no one felt excessively responsible for setting a test that would eliminate an option of concern to him or her alone. Each group member took personal responsibility for setting tests for the minimum standard of proof that enabled the group to be convinced, rather than tests designed to kill the option.

Test design on the remaining five options went smoothly, achieving ready agreement among all group members.

---

6) Conduct Analysis

Conducting the analysis prescribed by the test design brings in two key design features.

The first is what I call "the lazy man's approach to choice." This approach sequences the analytical testing of conditions in the reverse order of the group's confidence. That is, the condition the group feels least likely to hold up is tested first. If the group's suspicion is right, the relevant option (or options) will be eliminated without any of the other conditions being tested. If the group's suspicion is proven wrong, then the condition with the next lowest likelihood of confirmation is tested, and so on.

Since testing is often the most expensive and time-consuming part of the choice process, this lazy man's approach can save enormous amounts of resources. If an average option has four or five barrier conditions that must be tested, the lazy man's approach, by going to the harshest first, on average reduces the testing to two or three conditions.

Second, the key design feature is that the member of the group who is most skeptical that the test will confirm the condition oversees each analysis. This assures the skeptic that the test is being carried out using rigorous standards. If the skeptic comes back to the group saying that the analytical test has confirmed the condition, then the whole group will find the result compelling.

The broadest option and the most narrowly focused product option were the two the team was most skeptical about, so these two were tested first and eliminated. The sell option was set aside as the last resort, to be explored in more detail only if no other option was found to be feasible.

That left two options in active consideration. The first involved shrinking to three businesses: the wealth management market for higher-income, higher net worth individuals; electronic banking for retail customers broadly; and the small business market. The second option involved getting out of the manufacturing of financial products (for example, mutual funds, mortgages, loans, and so on) and becoming a broad-based distributor of third-party products using an advanced electronic banking platform.

7) Make Choice

Now it's time to make a choice—usually the most difficult, acrimonious, and time-consuming part of the entire process. The setting for these meetings is usually off-site, with participants surrounded by binders of analyses. In the past, these meetings tried to frame and make choices in one fell swoop. With the stakes high and the Ladders of Inference obscure, this is a fertile breeding ground for the Responsibility Virus. In the past, such conversations threatened all the governing values by way of defeat, loss of control, embarrassment, or loss of rationality. The participants chose either to withdraw and wait for the opportunity to passively resist later or to seize control to try to drive through to their desired conclusion.

But with the Choice Structuring Process, the choice-making step becomes a simple, anti-climactic step. The group has a shared understanding of the logic structure underpinning each option. The group has designed tests for each condition that act as a barrier to choice. For each condition, the most skeptical member has set the standard of proof and has overseen the analytical test.

The group needs only to review the analytical test results and make the choice dictated in advance by the particular pattern of test results. In essence, the choice is pre-sold; there is no need for serious debate at this late juncture. And there is no cause for the Virus to flare up, because the governing values are not threatened.

At FBC, the critical test of the distribution option was whether the margins in that business were sufficient to maintain acceptable profitability without the manufacturing businesses. They weren't, and this eliminated the distribution option and focused the group on the viability of the wealth management/electronic banking/small business option.

Rigorous testing validated the conditions of this option. The group approved this option at its final meeting. There was little acrimony, only resolve to go forward and make the strategy work. In contrast to the feelings of members at the outset, the group now felt like a team. They had a renewed sense of confidence that they could work together productively to solve the challenges that faced them.

CHAPTER 8

The Frame Experiment

Carrie is typical of Strategy Partners Incorporated consultants—high achievers from the finest colleges and the leading business schools, accustomed to being told they are the best and brightest, and unaccustomed to failure.

After growing up in a working-class family in Maine, Carrie, an attractive and intelligent woman, became the talk of her small town by gaining admission to Yale and with hard work and diligence graduating near the top of her class. Able to pick among competing offers at graduation, she started as an equity analyst at a Boston investment management firm.

It wasn't long, however, before she became frustrated by the progress of her career, and she left for the Harvard Business School, where she developed a passion for strategy consulting. Unlike the investment firm, this business would require her to use every last neuron in her brain. It offered the chance to work on the most challenging client problems and to really make a difference.

Of all the strategy firms, SPI was most attractive to Carrie because of its unique consulting philosophy, namely that active collaboration enhances clients' learning, at the same time that it ensures that their knowledge is fully brought to bear in creating solutions. SPI did not just plop down a fat report on the client's desk at the end of an assignment. On the typical SPI project, the clients discuss the targeted problem extensively with the consultant and they define desired outputs together. They form a joint team to develop a joint workplan, dividing up the project tasks between SPI consultants and members of the client staff.

In her interview with SPI, Carrie's only worry was that her small-town Maine background might hurt her chances, but to her great delight she received an offer and accepted it on the spot.

For her first three years at SPI, everything went well. Carrie served under experienced case leaders and she was known as a tireless worker who always did everything well and on time.

But things have become trickier now that Carrie has become a case leader herself. At thirty-five, Carrie finds herself wondering for the first time whether she's cut out for this business. She has a relatively junior case team working on a difficult and time-sensitive project. And things are not going well.

During the initial planning meetings, Carrie got the sense that the client team members were out of their depth in terms of the types of tasks and the fast pace of work required. Despite the frightened looks on their faces, she held firm to SPI's tradition of client involvement and tried to weave them into the process.

Now she wonders about her judgment. In the initial phase of the collaboration, the team members from the client side consistently failed in their tasks, and the failure now threatens to jeopardize the entire project. Carrie has never failed at anything and she's not about to start now.

She decides to seize the reins, but she rationalizes her decision by telling herself, "We're facing a tense situation. We're all in danger of taking a huge and very public fall. As the only person who can pull this out of the fire, I have to take charge. But I have to do it as quietly as possible to protect their egos. I don't want the client's people feeling down-in-the-mouth."

Carrie reconfigures the workplan to minimize the difficulty of what the client members are asked to do, relegating them to fairly simple data collection. The more complicated work is reassigned to the SPI team members, with Carrie taking on the lion's share. The schedule is not extended to reflect the failures in the first phase of the work, lest the client CEO see that as under-performance.

The client team members breathe a collective sigh of relief and accept all the changes with enthusiasm. They knew things were not going well and they are only too happy to have an excuse to distance themselves from the taint of a major bollix. In fact, they feel like the weight of the world has been lifted off their shoulders. They now look forward to a successful project with Carrie fully in control.

Their passive acceptance does not exactly raise them in Carrie's esteem. "Just as I thought," she tells herself. "They're not really committed. They're happy to take a free ride on my back. Well, that's why I'm on the fast track and they aren't!" She begins to treat the client team members as excess baggage. When they offer their help or sympathy, Carrie can barely conceal her contempt. She gives the distinct impression that every second she spends answering their questions is time stolen from the real work. Her haughtiness makes them back off further. They begin to resent Carrie for being unilateral and controlling, which mirrors her resentment of them for their "bad attitude" about the project and for being what she views as "hangers-on."

Doing their work as well as her own, Carrie inevitably stumbles under the weight. She misses a key deadline. At the postponed presentation she is chastised for poor progress, despite being given more time. After the meeting, the client CEO and Carrie's boss have a private huddle.

"Carrie, the client is pretty upset," her grim-faced boss tells her afterward. "He's not just upset about the missed deadline. It turns out his people are in revolt. They say you pushed them out of the picture and seized control. In their view, you're a control freak, and credit-hungry to boot. They feel that had they been properly deployed, they could have met the deadlines and the quality would have been fine. This is a serious matter, Carrie."

"What ingratitude!" thinks Carrie to herself. "Fine. You take charge. I could use a break." She builds an argument to her boss that the job was impossible, the client was lazy, and in that context the progress she made was really quite remarkable. But Carrie agrees to meet with the client team to hear their concerns and give them the lead role on the project going forward. Her boss reluctantly decides to give Carrie a second chance. Secretly, though, he wonders if Carrie is truly committed to the SPI way of consulting.

In the previous chapter we described a group process for structuring choices that wards off the Responsibility Virus. This tool succeeds by ensuring safeguards against violating the governing values of *win, don't lose; maintain control; avoid embarrassment;* and *stay rational.*

But sometimes, as in Carrie's case, it's too late for protection. The Virus already infects us. Misunderstanding and mistrust have already undermined collaboration, and our choice process is in terrible shape. This is when we need the Frame Experiment, a remedial tool for fighting the Virus and mending the frayed relationship.

The Responsibility Virus in Full Swing

Carrie's "fight" reaction, and the client team's "flight" reaction, both responses to the same fear of failure and the same assault on the governing values, should be familiar to you by now.

In the wake of the problems at the very beginning of the case, Carrie fears not just losing but losing control, and then losing face by being thoroughly embarrassed. When her fear reaches a threshold level, her instincts take over. At this point her actions cannot be considered rational, or well-reasoned, much less optimal.

In Carrie's construction of the situation, she has to "fight" by pre-emptively and unilaterally seizing control because the client team gave her no choice. By blaming them she wins regardless of the outcome. Since she chooses to fight, she maintains control. Since she does so unilaterally and without conversation, she avoids the embarrassment of telling the client team members that their incompetence was at the root of the problems. Of course, taking the step unilaterally also helps Carrie avoid an awkward conversation with the client members about her failure to adhere to SPI's stated values. And finally, even though emotions seethe through her being, she makes highly rational arguments to herself, her team, and the client as to why the change is "optimal."

Faced with the same fear of failure, the client team members experience their automatic "flight" reaction. As Carrie seizes control, they back off and set the bar low enough to ensure victory, manage a narrowly defined and doable task to keep fully in control, and avoid revealing that they were not up to the previous task. By withdrawing unilaterally and not challenging Carrie's recasting of the workplan, they also avoid an embarrassing discussion about the decision to withdraw. In addition, they feel comfortable holding Carrie entirely responsible for success because she seized the reins of her own accord. By their reasoning they had no rational choice but to concur.

Their unilateral decision to withdraw ensconces Carrie's over-responsibility, while at the same time it convinces her that she was correct in her assessment of the clients' weak capabilities. Yet when her over-responsibility produces failure, Carrie's fight strategy falls apart and she switches to flight. She, too, withdraws in order to avoid the humiliation of failure.

Reflecting on Our Frames

The Responsibility Virus creates in each party the impression that the other players are progressively more extreme and negative. For us to maintain adherence to our governing values, the other party must, in our view, increasingly take on a specific set of negative attributes. Carrie sees the client team members as increasingly lazy, disingenuous, and pathetic. They see Carrie as increasingly controlling, domineering, and sarcastic.

These negative attributes get embodied in an internally consistent view of the world, which we take into subsequent interactions. This mental construct guides the way we select and process data in a given situation. The key parts of this way of framing reality are:

1. the view of the task at hand,
2. the view of one's self with respect to the task, and
3. the view of the other with respect to the task.

In the case of Carrie, after the initial problems in the case, she framed *her task* as being to take control of the project. In this mental construct *she* was the last best hope for the case and the only one who could see the problems and solutions. *The client team members* were to accept passively and gratefully the wisdom of her insight.

A frame is the most general description of such a knowledge structure. It is a way of seeing a particular situation—a way of making sense of the random collection of sense perceptions that make up a given predicament. Frames have been studied from numerous perspectives and are referred to variously as scripts,[1] metaphors,[2] and cognitive biases.[3] We might approach, for instance, a shareholders' meeting in the same way a gladiator approaches the arena—in a combative mindset—ready to go to great lengths to silence the "opposition." We might approach an impending marriage as a market transaction—attempting to set floors and ceilings on future gains and losses, by drafting meticulously constructed pre-nuptial agreements. We might approach an MBA class as a piece of entertainment—expecting to be passively entertained while information—and ideally knowledge—unobtrusively seeps into our minds.

Frames are an attempt to make sense of the world. They are a way to constrain our predicaments and subsequent judgments and actions. But these frames take on a special power because we hold them unconsciously—even though they reflect themselves in our everyday language—and we allow them to shape our perceptions of events.[4] They are "sticky" even when we do become conscious of them because we have a well-established tendency to discount evidence that counters the theories and models that we hold to be true.[5]

For these reasons, our frames hold us for ransom: we can be rid of them only if we are willing to undergo the pain of having our deepest intuitions and assumptions open to refutation by the criticism of others—a pain that we are often not able to endure.[6] This leads us to stick to our frames and models even when they are no longer useful. For this reason, for us to take remedial action against the Responsibility Virus, we must reflect upon and alter the frame that contributed to its introduction, even if it feels scary and painful.

Our frames originate with our governing values, which produce consistent and counterproductive ways of framing the world in general. The most dominant frame is driven by our governing values, as illustrated in Figure 8.1.

The governing value of *win, don't lose* causes us to see ourselves as knowing the right answer and to see the other individual as uninformed. Or worse, we may see the other individual as threatening to win or harboring some ill-intentioned purpose. The value *maintain control* causes us to see the task as getting the other to come to our point of view. And the values *avoid embarrassment* and *stay rational* guide us to act on the frame in unilateral ways that minimize meaningful discussion.

However, each of us has a conception of ourselves in relation to others and to the world that causes us to create a frame to protect our governing values in our own characteristic way. It's like a footprint. For example, a puritanical upbringing could cause the self to be not only the one who

FIGURE 8.1   Dominant Frame

Governing Values	Frame
• Win, don't lose • Maintain control • Avoid embarrassment • Stay rational	• **Self:** I know the right answer • **Other Individual:** Is uninformed or ill-intentioned • **Task:** Get him/her to see things my way

knows the right answer, but also the only one honest enough to face up to that answer. The others in this framing may be more likely to be ill-intentioned—that is, too morally suspect to admit the truth—rather than uninformed. The task may then be shaded toward getting the others to see things "my" way, which is the only true, honest, and moral way. Or streetwise individuals may see themselves as knowing the right answer because they can see the relationships and coalitions and their behind-the-scenes impacts on what appears to be a straightforward negotiation. The others are uninformed because they are pathetically naive in thinking that it is just a negotiation about contract terms. The task for the streetwise individual is to make sure the naive fools don't screw up the deal by being clueless as to "what is really going on."

Carrie came to this case with a self-image of the hardworking, reliable consultant who had worked her way up from a humble upbringing through working harder and paying more attention to building her craft than anyone around her. This was her footprint and it made itself felt even in the initial planning meetings. Carrie wanted to make sure her design prevailed, because she was, after all, the knowledgeable consultant hired by the client to solve the problem, and creating a workplan was one of the skills she had worked hard to perfect. Yes, she would be collaborative, but that didn't imply a free-for-all in the planning meeting—"I know the right answer" was a condition that needed to hold up.

In a parallel—though bizarre—fashion the frame also held up from the client side. Client team members knew that they were right about what they could and could not do and were confident that Carrie was uninformed and would make mistakes. However, they were willing to wait until Carrie failed for her to see things their way.

When the fear of failure skyrocketed after the first phase, Carrie's framing maintained the same structure but became more harshly negative. Now, she was absolutely right and the client team members were not just uninformed but ill-intentioned. The frame expanded to include the belief that they were lazy, disingenuous, and out to make her life miserable. She had to get these people to cooperate or they would destroy the project and hurt her career.

Similarly, as Carrie's frame became more severe, so did the frames of the client team members. They saw Carrie as ill-intentioned, as well as uninformed. She was a bully, not interested in them, not empathetic, and not a nice human being.

As the Virus progresses, the frame becomes more punitive, conditioning the way each action by every player is interpreted. The inferences become ever more self-contained and self-reflexive. Any new data is interpreted in a fashion that is consistent with the existing frame. Any inconsistent data is ignored or dismissed as invalid or non-representative. In this way, the frame is automatically reinforced. Sadly, there is no way for it to be disconfirmed because all potentially disconfirming data is ignored or dismissed. It is hermetically sealed against contradiction.

Once the frame becomes fully sealed off, it drives the Responsibility Virus to its logical extreme. The parties migrate to ever more over-responsible and under-responsible stances, consistent with the framing of one another as, in turn, domineering or pathetic. By the time of the crisis meeting with the CEO and Carrie's boss, Carrie sees the client team members as utterly incompetent and maliciously intentioned, while the client team members see Carrie as controlling, selfish, and mean-spirited.

In the various cases—Michael and Caroline at *Wapshot*, Pierre and Hakeem at the IDA, Dwight and Harry at White & Jeffries, Ned and Dick at STG—the frames became ever more tightly sealed off against reality as the Responsibility Virus took hold. There was little or no chance of the parties avoiding the drift into more extreme positions of over- or under-responsibility. In all the cases, the self-sealing and counterproductive frames helped drive the situation into crisis.

The Frame Experiment

The tool for breaking out of this self-sealing loop is called *The Frame Experiment*. It was created by Diana Smith, a founder of a consulting firm called Action Design.[7] Unlike the Choice Structuring Process, which is designed to keep the parties from getting into trouble, this is a remedial tool designed to help you recover.

The Frame Experiment does not attempt to cure the Virus at once. Instead it is designed to arrest the self-sealing downward spiral of worsening frames and provide the opportunity for an upward spiral to take shape. In a Frame Experiment, I ask the individual to employ an alternative, more productive frame.

The existing frame sees *self* as knowing the right answer, the *other individual* as not getting it, and the *task at hand* as getting the other to see things "my way." At first, the individual is inclined to vigorously deny that this frame represents his or her thinking because it seems so blatantly ill-intentioned. However, when the participants reflect on this characterization more, they tend to realize that it is accurate. It may not be particularly nice, but it is accurate. More important, they see how every move they make derives directly from this frame.

In the Frame Experiment, I work with the individual to develop an altered frame about self, the other individual, and the task at hand in the interaction.

The altered frame is not completely different from the existing frame, but the differences drive significant, positive changes. The frame of *self* changes from knowing the right answer to having an important point of view. It makes a simple adjustment that leaves the door open a tiny crack to additional insight: the self *may not* see or understand *everything*. The altered frame does not actually assume the self is missing anything. It only introduces this as a possibility, and a possibility worth taking into account.

Why is this so important? Because it drives curiosity. With the belief that "I know the right answer," there is no room for further growth in understanding. With no curiosity, the views of others have no merit and others have no utility. They become, as in the view of Carrie, hangers-on. With "I may not see or understand everything," there is still interest in the unknown territory and in the views of others that may—not necessarily do—have value.

FIGURE 8.2   Frame Experiment

Existing Frame	Altered Frame
• Self: I know the right answer	**• Self:** I have a wealth of data and experience, but I may not see or understand everything
• Other Individual: Is uninformed or ill-intentioned	**• Other Individual:** He/she may see things that I don't see which may contribute to my understanding
• Task: Get him/her to see things my way	**• Task:** Access our collective intelligence in order to make the best choice

In similar fashion, the reframing of the other person opens the door a tiny crack. The other *may* see things that the self doesn't, which *may* contribute to understanding. This is a qualified stance. The other individual may not have anything whatsoever to add, but this leaves the possibility open that they may. The data to which they have access and the inferences that they draw may be different, and by being different, they may contribute in some way.

Why is this qualified opening important? Because it encourages inquiry into the other person's point of view. This draws the others into taking responsibility rather than pushing them away from doing so.

Finally, the task at hand changes, in this case by the most significant margin. It changes from persuading the other to change his or her mind to accessing the collective intelligence. That is, it seeks to access the combined data pools of self and other and to utilize the inference-drawing capabilities of both parties. However, the altered task does not assume that the other party will contribute anything useful. It simply remains open to the possibility that there might be a contribution that goes beyond the data and reasoning of the self.

This change is important because it also has the effect of drawing the other persons into the task at hand rather than making them feel pushed out and overruled. It acknowledges that both parties may have something important to contribute. And they probably, though not certainly, do.

The altered frame is not easy for the self to implement, and because it is ambiguous, it causes tension with respect to the governing values. The altered frame does not feel completely like *winning, not losing*. And leaving open the possibility that the other party will contribute can feel like undermining control. So the individual approaches the Frame Experiment with some queasiness. However, *queasiness* is an improvement over outright fear. Because the possibility of some embarrassment persists, when I use the Frame Experiment, I ask the individual to try it for just one specific interaction, one for which they can plan in advance.

I want it to feel like a baby step, not a giant leap. By limiting the scope of the Frame Experiment to just one interaction, I lower the level of queasiness. If the individuals feel they are losing, getting out of control, or risking embarrassment, they can drop the experiment after the one interaction and go back to whatever they had been doing.

Applying the experiment to a planned interaction enables the individual to take the time to thoroughly adopt the altered frame before entering the conversation. They can think about each aspect of the altered frame and personalize it to the other individual. That is: *Bob may see something I am missing. Bob's insights may contribute to my understanding. Bob and I may be able to come up with a better answer than I could on my own.*

Despite all the preparation, a characteristic fear typically remains. Given the *win, don't lose* value that is so deeply ingrained, the individual fears that the other party will see the frame as a sign of weakness and will exploit that weakness to his advantage. So I give the individual an additional out.

I ask him to try the Frame Experiment only for the first five minutes of the interaction. If after five minutes, he finds himself in trouble or feeling uneasy, he can return to his old frame and continue the conversation.

Universally, they find this to be an acceptable bargain. All the Frame Experiment asks is that they leave the door open for five minutes. Many suspect that the other will behave badly given the opportunity, and validate the accuracy of their original frame. But by asking for so little, I get them to humor me.

However, when they try the experiment, a surprising thing usually happens. The other party *doesn't* behave badly. They are inspired by the open and cooperative behavior of my experimenter. The other party *does* see things my experimenter didn't see or understand. And these things *do* contribute meaningfully to their understanding. And they *do*, with the help of the other individual, come up with a better choice. My experimenter finds it progressively easy during the interaction to maintain the altered frame. In fact, they find the old frame becoming increasingly inappropriate. In the end, they typically wonder what on earth led them to hold this intelligent, useful other person in such low esteem prior to the conversation.

All of which suggests, once again, that it takes two to tango. Static conservation of responsibility holds. The instant one party decides *not* to either seize control or retreat into passivity, the other party is invited into a real conversation. And it is a compelling invitation. The other party lacks the energy to take an extreme position because the experimenter doesn't supply the energy by seizing or abdicating responsibility. There is no apparent threat to the governing values. There is therefore no incentive and little capability to behave badly.

Participants typically emerge from the Frame Experiment on an emotional high. I routinely have individuals coming out of their first Frame Experiment claiming that this represented the best meeting of their business careers. The level of mutual learning, the quality of the thinking, and the newly apparent intelligence of their partner is a wholly positive revelation.

It also feels wonderful for experimenters to see the downward spiral in a relationship arrested, then turned into the beginnings of an upward spiral of trust, understanding, and mutual benefit. They come out of the Frame Experiment willing, if not eager, to broaden the experiment. They most certainly go into the next conversation holding the altered frame. And the fact that the two parties work together productively and intelligently during the conversation itself prompts them to share responsibilities coming out of the conversation.

My experience with the Frame Experiment is one of overwhelming success. Only in a small minority of cases does it not work brilliantly. And never has it failed so thoroughly as to make the situation worse. The positive results provide sufficient encouragement to the individual to broaden the experiment to other meetings and other relationships. With each experiment, confidence grows and ability to take remedial action against the Responsibility Virus heightens.

CHAPTER 9

The Responsibility Ladder

In early 1996, I was the one trying to fend off the Virus. A year and a half earlier, I had taken over as chief operating officer of my consulting firm. The firm had thirteen offices worldwide and about 1,000 full-time employees. I had taken on a crushing level of responsibility and knew that I would burn out if I didn't make some adjustments. In my colleagues I noticed the same "under-responsible" behaviors that had confronted my client senior executives. Worse, I was taking off on the same "over-responsible" death march that had threatened to undo many of these same leaders.

"We have a big problem with receivables collection," I'd hear from Brenda, the head of finance. Then she would listen, waiting for me to suggest a course of action, which I obligingly did, implicitly taking on 100 percent of the responsibility for fixing the problem.

Sam, the head of IT, would enter on what appeared at first blush to be a more responsible footing, saying: "Roger, we have real vulnerability in security for our global voice and data network. I recommend we hire someone full-time as soon as possible. But we don't have room in the budget. Is it OK anyway?" At first I thought: "Great. He's coming with both the problem—security vulnerability—and a solution—hiring someone." However, after mulling it over I realized that the problem wasn't the security of the network, which he was handling, but the difficult budget tradeoff that he was dumping on me.

And I had problems at the other end of the spectrum as well. Frank, the head of consulting services, would take unilateral actions that would make me cringe when he reported them to me. Once he informed me, after it was too late to change, that he had unilaterally canceled an extremely popular year-end employee recognition program, for vague reasons that, to me, made no sense.

Brenda and Sam were taking on far too little responsibility and Frank was taking too much, while other members of the management team vacillated back and forth. I noticed that I was defaulting to the same standard, which was implicitly encouraging this behavior. I either unilaterally determined that a given manager was not up to a task and took over myself, or I assumed that they were capable and left them alone. I found myself overwhelmed with the amount of work I faced. In time, I realized that I would crash and burn if I didn't change my behavior and the behavior of my managers.

I convened the group to talk about approaches to sharing responsibility. Our first initiative was the establishment of protocols that set out my responsibilities against the collective responsibilities of the management team. However, this approach was too blunt in two respects.

First, all issues or problems were not identical and therefore one standard division of responsibilities between my managers and me could not apply. For tough problems involving overall firm policy, I needed to take more than the generic level of responsibility suggested in the draft system. For easier problems in an individual manager's domain, I needed to take less responsibility than standard.

Second, each manager was operating from a somewhat different stage of personal development. The more experienced managers were capable of taking more problem-solving responsibility than the least developed managers.

A fixed set of rules came up short on both counts; instead, we developed something called the Responsibility Ladder. It was designed to be a flexible tool for organizing problem-solving conversations rather than for dictating their outcomes. The Ladder became our primary management tool for navigating our working relationship.

While Choice Structuring is a process tool, and the Frame Experiment is a remedial tool, the Responsibility Ladder is a development tool for improving choice-making capabilities. It is a way of structuring conversations that will yield a better distribution of responsibilities, thus inoculating us against the Responsibility Virus.

The Need to Transform Conversations on the Distribution of Responsibility

At the heart of the Responsibility Virus are unproductive conversations—and often non-conversations—about the distribution of responsibility for decisions. The governing values of *win, don't lose, maintain control, avoid embarrassment,* and *stay rational* produce the frame of *I'm right, they're wrong and my task is to get them to see the light.*

The values and the frame create a context that makes such conversations difficult, uncomfortable, and potentially embarrassing. The self-protective, anxiety-minimizing solution is to pretend to have real conversations while in fact hiding behind interpersonal maneuvers aimed at maintaining everyone's self-enhancing routines.

The purpose of responsibility conversations should not be to determine who's in charge but to divide tasks so that the responsibilities assigned to each party match each party's capabilities. This is the only way to maximize the choice-making development of each individual.

These conversations also should build internal commitment and accountability for the responsibility assumed. And finally, they should develop in the parties involved a sense of collaboration and mutual support with respect to their overall, collective goals.

But such conversations require a more sophisticated language system, one that goes beyond the binary possibilities of "I'm in charge" or "you're in charge" to encompass a more subtle, graduated scale of responsibility. Only by accommodating shades of gray can we talk productively through the division of tasks.

A more nuanced vocabulary is also what's needed to discuss the subtle increases in responsibility level that are consistent with capability growth. The vocabulary of all or nothing—either "you're in charge" or "I'm in charge"—limits personal growth options to huge leaps that often lead to painful failures.

The Responsibility Ladder

The language of the Responsibility Ladder accommodates six graduated levels, each of which we may adopt as our part in the overall responsibility for solving a problem. While levels of responsibility no doubt could be parsed in any number of ways, in my experience, these six are the key levels to which most people gravitate in most situations. Thus the rungs on the ladder are designed to represent the natural break points in taking responsibility for choice-making, moving from lowest to highest.

The lowest rung on the ladder, Level 6, involves taking on no responsibility, the classic dumping of a problem onto the lap of another, most often one's superior. We've all experienced a subordinate coming in to inform us that something terrible has happened, then standing there, wide-eyed, waiting for us to make some decision and not lifting a finger to help. This is hardly ever an appropriate level of responsibility. True, I would rather have my eleven-year-old tell me that the dog has pooped on the carpet than to try to clean it up by himself, but I am not so enthusiastic about having my CFO tell me we have a receivables problem and take less initiative than my eleven-year-old with the dog mess.

Level 5 appears almost identical to Level 6, but there is an important difference: you make it clear that you will apply to the next case whatever you might learn from the other party's involvement this time. This is acceptance of an additional level of responsibility, even though it applies to the next choice. It encourages the other parties to believe that they will not be asked to assume total responsibility on an ongoing basis. It signals a willingness and interest in developing choice-making capabilities in order to share a greater portion of the burden going forward.

This small signal can help stave off a Responsibility Virus infection. The person on the receiving end is more likely to explain their reasoning in tackling the problem presented, in hope, perhaps, that the reasoning will be applied to future similar situations. Generally speaking, they will also treat the

FIGURE 9.1   The Responsibility Ladder

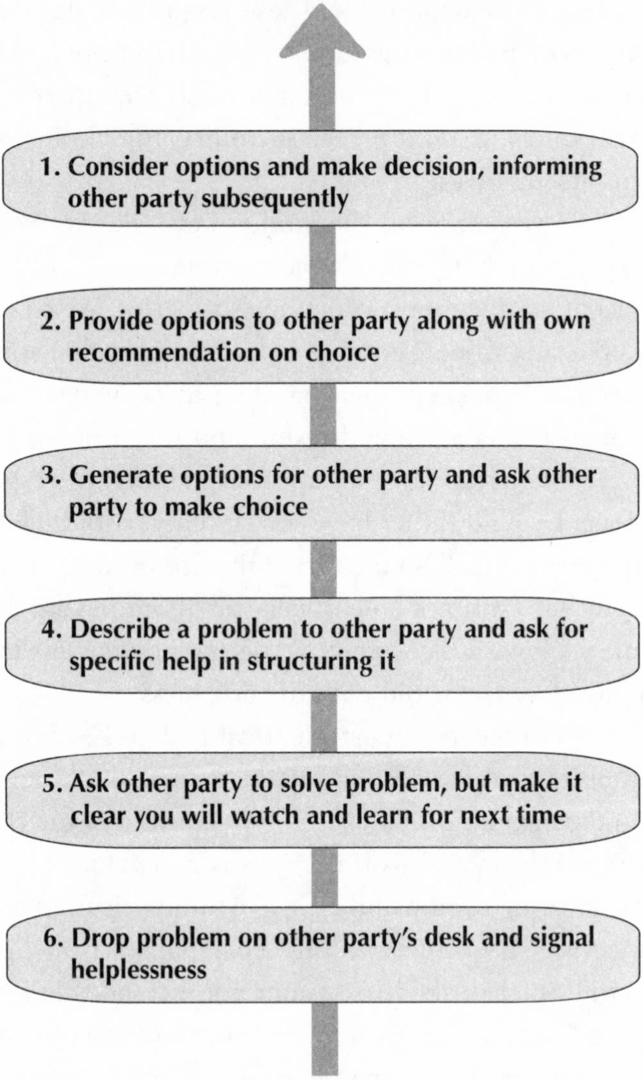

1. Consider options and make decision, informing other party subsequently

2. Provide options to other party along with own recommendation on choice

3. Generate options for other party and ask other party to make choice

4. Describe a problem to other party and ask for specific help in structuring it

5. Ask other party to solve problem, but make it clear you will watch and learn for next time

6. Drop problem on other party's desk and signal helplessness

person taking Level 5 responsibility with considerably more respect than if they had taken a strict Level 6 stance.

At Level 4, the individual asks the other party for help in structuring the issue or task. Problem structuring is the most abstract part of choice-making, and thus the most difficult. The key issue is how to think about the choice at hand. In the language of the Choice Structuring Process, this is the step that takes a vaguely defined problem or issue and frames it as a choice among mutually exclusive options. At this level, the individual signals to the other party that he or she doesn't want the other party to simply take over and make the choice. Instead the individual wants to participate with the other party as he or she leads in the structuring. Once again, this level signals a desire to collaborate rather than to fade into the background.

At Level 3, the individual takes on responsibility for structuring the choice and developing options, but still does not feel capable of coming up with a recommended choice from among the options. This level of responsibility feels much more supportive from the perspective of a boss. At this level, the subordinate is saying: "I have noticed a problem, I've thought about it, and I think there are four options for dealing with it. What do you think?" As we all know, that goes down a lot better than: "I've noticed a problem. What are you going to do about it?"

At Level 2, the individual feels capable of analyzing the options and coming forward to the other party with a recommendation. At this level, the individual is not sufficiently confident in his or her choice-making capabilities to make the decision and accept the consequences, but he or she is sufficiently confident to go beyond enumeration of options to recommending an option. At Level 2, the individual is taking on a large portion of the decisionmaking responsibility, even if the other party (most likely the boss) takes responsibility for making the final choice. Those who operate at Level 2 may be subordinates, but we tend to treat them as colleagues.

At Level 1, after having structured the choice, generated options, analyzed the options, and made the final decision, the individual operates unilaterally. Their only interaction with the other party is to inform them of the choice they have made. In a boss-subordinate relationship, when the subordinate consistently operates successfully in a Level 1 mode, it is a signal that this person should no longer be a subordinate. Such an elevation not only stretches that person's capabilities, it gives his or her former superior more time to dedicate to managing others.

Although Levels 1 through 6 are available to us in virtually all of our joint choice-making situations, unfortunately we take on either Level 1 or Level 6 responsibility in the vast majority of cases.

Level 1 is the traditional definition of heroic leadership. It screams "I'm in charge" and implies "you had better get out of the way."

Level 6 warns that the other person had better step forward or else the choice won't get made and whatever problem spurred the choice will get worse, not better.

In most cases, neither Level 1 nor Level 6 is accurately correlated with our actual capabilities. That discrepancy leads the other party, and us, into reflexive over- or under-responsibility. Either one signals an outbreak of the Responsibility Virus.

Levels 1 and 6 also require the least interaction and relationship building. Operating in these levels reinforces the negative frames that feed the Virus and undermine any inclination to collaborate.

By contrast, taking responsibility in the range of Levels 2 through 5 causes the parties to work and think together, which has the effect of building relationships, growing positive frames, and inoculating against the Virus.

Levels 2 through 5 are where we want to be most of the time, but it is very difficult even to talk about such graduated steps in the current language of responsibility. In fact, the language of "empowerment" currently in vogue implicitly encourages individuals and groups with few relevant capabilities and little practical experience to seize Level 1 responsibility. Some "empowered" individuals are clever enough to realize that they are not ready for that kind of autonomy. Unfortunately, the experience tends to convince them that the bosses who encouraged empowerment are either disingenuous or clueless or both.

Sadly, bosses who strive for empowerment become convinced that the objects of their efforts are uncooperative and retrograde. Others, who are not so clever, take on the empowered responsibility, fail, and then blame the bosses, who appear to have set them up for failure. The bosses in turn come to believe that empowerment can't work because of their employees' inherently low capacity for taking on responsibility.

Using the Responsibility Ladder

The Responsibility Ladder provides the language and structure necessary to reach agreement on intermediate levels of responsibility in which manager and subordinate truly share in the task of solving the problem at hand. It provides both of them ready access to Levels 2 through 5, which enables the more accurate matching of responsibilities to capabilities. It also supports development by giving the participants benchmarks of responsibility, allowing them to chart their progress as their capabilities build.

Used prospectively, the Ladder enables a finely tuned conversation that allows for more precise adjustments to responsibilities as capabilities grow. And it helps overcome classic problems subordinates encounter when taking on responsibilities.

Typically, subordinates face a dilemma when they feel nervous about taking on something new. They can either: 1) Cover up the nervousness and accept the assignment, committing to an effort that will probably fail; or 2) Admit nervousness, be viewed as incapable, and be shunted aside. If they are inclined to delay trouble, they will probably pick the former. If they are inclined to exhibit their nervousness and allow others to decide for them, they will choose the latter. The subordinates fear—with reason—that their superiors are on hair-triggers, and that any flinch on their part may result in seizure of responsibility by the boss.

With the Responsibility Ladder, the boss can avoid subjecting the subordinate to this all-or-nothing dilemma by providing a menu of levels. The existence of this explicit range causes the subordinates to feel a greater sense of comfort with their feelings and to feel less of a sense that they need to cover up or express nervousness. It also provides a useful context for discussing those feelings in concrete terms.

This feeling of comfort is tremendously important to the individual, who must override his or her traditional governing values to even engage in this conversation. This interaction can guide the subordinate to a level of responsibility that is consistent with capabilities and enable the boss to be both confident and balanced in his or her own responsibilities.

The Responsibility Ladder also can be used retrospectively to diagnose failure and learn from it, rather than engaging in unproductive recrimination. Instead of despairing at the point of failure, the parties can explore what levels of responsibility they each accepted and why that allocation of responsibilities failed. By doing so, they can avoid the sweeping generalizations and arbitrary fixes that usually follow failures. Arbitrary fixes rarely enhance the development of capabilities. The Ladder is not a benchmark for growth; it creates the context for a productive conversation about subtle modifications that help avoid future failures.

The goal of each of us should be to increase our choice-making capability and take on more responsibility, as appropriate, over time. Since capabilities do not typically grow in giant leaps but in small increments (whether quickly or slowly), responsibilities should grow incrementally as well. The Responsibility Ladder offers a tremendous tool for personal development to substitute for the current language of leadership, which assigns new responsibilities in all-or-nothing steps.

In the context of the discrete assignment, a superior makes a binary decision that a subordinate "can handle it" or is "not ready for it," language that works against the smooth ramping up of responsibilities. The subordinate is either deemed not ready for it for too long and never receives the appropriate opportunities for learning, or one day the decision comes down that, suddenly, they "can handle it," which forces them to step into much bigger shoes all at once.

Owing to rigid job definitions in most organizations, individuals stay in their current jobs too long, coasting at their existing capability level, then get bumped up to a level for which they are often unprepared. As a result, most of us spend the majority of our careers either coasting at responsibility levels below our capabilities or being terrified by responsibility levels above our capabilities. This vacillation slows our growth in ways we don't even recognize.

Use of the Responsibility Ladder helps us understand our responsibility progression over time. This not only reduces the incidence of the Virus, but it speeds the pace of personal development. The small steps provided by the Ladder smooth the transitions, making it unnecessary to take on too much or too little responsibility. The steps also provide us with benchmarks to measure our progress. We can try one step higher when we see that we have been able to master the step below. Such an incremental progress provides regular encouragement while reducing the fear of failure.

The Responsibility Ladder also enables us to have more subtle and sophisticated conversations that distinguish between types of tasks and appropriate responsibilities. While in general our progress in a given job should be mirrored by a general progression up the Responsibility Ladder (that is, taking on Level 2 responsibility rather than staying back at Level 3), all tasks are not equal in difficulty.

For each of us, Level 5 may be appropriate for a certain complicated task in which help from our superior is required, and Level 1 may be appropriate for another task for which we have good experience. These variations are often glossed over in job descriptions as well as in less formal conversations. But with the Responsibility Ladder the distinctions can be made clear. This allows the superior to provide targeted help to the subordinate in growing the skills required to move up the Ladder.

The Responsibility Ladder is most effective as a tool if a team whose members work together regularly uses it explicitly. Whenever apportioning responsibility for a choice, the team should use the steps of the Ladder as a mechanism for dividing the tasks. The goal of each member should be to move up the Ladder over time; a goal of their colleagues should be to help them in their progress. The conversations need not take long. In fact, they can be used to more quickly and efficiently assign roles and responsibilities within a group.

As COO, the Responsibility Ladder helped me improve the effectiveness of the management team members as well as my relationships with them. For example, it helped my relationship with Brenda, who was inclined to cover up nervousness and accept assignments she should not have taken on. Her resultant failures had undermined my confidence in her, which caused me to give her less and less responsibility. The Responsibility Ladder helped us have conversations that resulted in productive joint responsibility for initiatives. The conversations also helped her get assistance from other members of the management team.

Using the Responsibility Ladder retrospectively helped me particularly with Frank, who strained our relationship by his misguided propensity for adopting Level 1 responsibilities. The Ladder allowed us to calmly diagnose the failures created, and then develop a system for having productive conversations before Frank took any unilateral action.

Sam, the information technology head, was able to learn that behavior that felt quite responsible to him—for example, informing me of the data security problem and recommending hiring above his budget to solve the problem—was actually Level 6 behavior from my perspective. We were able to have conversations in which we settled on higher levels of responsibility for Sam for difficult tasks. In the case of the data security problems, Sam could have recommended budget adjustments to absorb the new expenditure without an increase in overall spending. That was well within his capabilities, and it would have represented a Level 2 apportionment.

We also developed shorthand by which Sam would start the conversation with: "I think this is a Level 2 situation." The technique dramatically enhanced the speed and efficiency of our problem-solving conversations. It also enabled me to get myself into the proper mindset quickly and avoid having to guess where this conversation was taking us. At the end of the conversation, we were able to reflect on Sam's initial assumption. Was he aiming too low or too high from the outset? What led him to do so? What role did I play in his choice?

With Les, the head of training, the Responsibility Ladder helped him to overcome a tendency to undershoot his responsibility by one level. Perhaps because his early training was in a big bureaucratic organization, he had a greater fear of taking on one incremental level of responsibility too much and failing than he did of the consequence of slowing his own development by taking on one level too little. Les would come to me with a recommendation when he should have made a decision himself, or he'd come to me with options when actually he felt quite strongly about a recommendation. Using the Responsibility Ladder, I encouraged him to take more of what felt to him like risks. He began to reach higher in order to build his capabilities. Equally important, Les helped me understand what I could do to support him in this effort.

The Responsibility Ladder helped Trish, the head of recruiting, who was probably the most capable in her job, take the final steps necessary to act independently. Trish was close to that level but didn't really understand how to conceptualize what it would take to achieve an independent state. The Responsibility Ladder helped us determine in which areas she operated at below Level 1 and to target those areas for joint work at developing her capabilities and confidence. Without the framework of the Responsibility Ladder, it would have been difficult for Trish and me to have those conversations or home in on her key development needs.

But very likely I was the person who benefited most from the Responsibility Ladder. By progressively taking on more responsibility, and thereby encouraging my team to take on less, I was setting myself up for a failure that would bring my team down with me. The Responsibility Ladder enabled me to have individual and group conversations to effect a net transfer of responsibilities from me to the members of the management team. With one exception, the team members were able to make the transition, aided by the smooth progression and benchmarking of the Responsibility Ladder.

Thanks to the more precise definition of levels, we were able to come to decisions on responsibility much more quickly. We would reference the step we were considering taking and that shorthand would quickly put the parties on the same page. In my busy world, this timesaving was invaluable.

Another benefit of the Responsibility Ladder was that it reframed the very idea of dispersion of responsibility. The question was no longer one of bilateral apportionment between a single team member and myself but rather a multilateral apportionment. The Ladder helped us place any given responsibility in the hands of the most appropriate individual, which made the team feel more like a team. And finally, as a leader, I felt less alone, less inclined to leap into over-responsibility at the slightest provocation.

All of the above notwithstanding, I was too far along the path of over-responsibility by the time the Responsibility

Ladder came along. I burned out and, at the end of the year, resigned as COO to return to full-time consulting. Nonetheless, I had learned two powerful lessons: how to manage responsibility levels in myself, and how to help my team members manage themselves going forward.

10

The Redefinition
of Leadership
and Followership

Head of strategy for WorldNet, a giant global telecommunications firm, Henry is, at forty-two, almost a decade younger than the other executive vice presidents. He's a lifelong runner who hates to miss his morning miles. And he works the same way that he runs, fast and furious, with a steady stream of executives bustling in and out of his office every day.

Early in his career Henry was identified as a candidate with high potential. Fed on a steady diet of challenging assignments, he demonstrated that he had the "total package." He was great in sales, where his outgoing, gregarious, and genuine demeanor was a hit with customers. He was a breath of fresh air during his time in network operations, where his powerful intellect helped cut through complex technical problems. In marketing, he had taken a

sophisticated, analytical approach to segmenting and understanding the customer base, and in doing so, he fundamentally changed the way WorldNet approached its customers. Regardless of the setting, his subordinates loved
him for his upbeat, can-do approach and his human touch.

The current CEO, Nick, has begun treating Henry as a
confidante, perhaps even as heir apparent. A fatherly figure with a calm disposition, Nick had talked Henry
through his potential career path when he took over the
portfolio for strategy. Actually, Henry had been hoping for
one of the two big business unit presidencies, which were
clearly the route to the top. But Henry knew that would
have been a stretch. As was currently the case, those spots
typically were staffed with executives in their mid-fifties.
However, Nick explained to Henry that he had decided to
put him in charge of strategy as a way to broaden him and
keep him challenged without shunting aside the two significantly older and more experienced line business unit presidents. Organizationally, this top staff job was only one
step below business unit president, and Henry knew his
time would come.

But this nicely organized plan had a flaw. Bill, president of one of the two major business units, was struggling
and causing performance problems for WorldNet as a
whole. Nick called Henry into his office for a chat about
the problem.

"The job has just become too complicated for him,"
Nick admits, painfully. "But I really don't want to remove
him. It would just be too disruptive to the organization.
He's a good and loyal guy who's trying as hard as he can,
and I want to see him take early retirement in a couple of
years with his head held high. Why don't you start looking
out for him? Help him with some of the complicated items

on his plate, like the big alliance strategy and the whole capital planning mess. Don't tell him I've sent you. But if he comes to me to discuss your involvement, I'll support you. You won't get into any trouble with me for overstepping any bounds."

Without a moment's hesitation, Henry leaps into action. He could see the pain on Nick's face and he wanted it to go away. He also shared Nick's assessment of Bill. Everybody knew the man was in way over his head. He was from the "kinder and gentler" era in the business, when a firm handshake, a nice suit, and a good golf game were enough to produce a successful executive. There was a name for these types at WorldNet—42-Longs—referring to the suit size of a tall, fit executive. Yet Bill was causing big enough problems at WorldNet that Henry's stock option plan was feeling the pinch. "Besides," Henry tells himself, "this is the real test. When I pull this off, it'll be crystal clear that I'm ready for Bill's job."

Henry sits down with Bill and offers to "help" on a range of tasks. Bill is much wilier than either Henry or the CEO gives him credit for; contrary to their opinion, it takes more than a 42-Long build to get this far. It takes political skills as well, and Bill immediately recognizes Nick's shadow right behind Henry. "Far be it from me to reject my CEO's wisdom," he thinks. "If Nick thinks I need Henry's help, I'd better go along with it. In fact, I feel better already!"

On each task, Henry immediately seizes total control and races off to try to complete the job. Bill shrugs his shoulders and lets Henry take charge while he focuses on other, easier tasks. He knows in his heart that Henry is headed for trouble, but convinces himself not to cross swords with his boss.

Henry soon finds that doing his own job and much of Bill's, without public authority for the latter, is keeping him busier than he ever imagined. Bill's tasks are a bit trickier than they appeared from the outside and are taking a lot longer to get on top of. Things start falling through the cracks as Henry races from assignment to assignment. Henry's reputation for thoroughness, dependability, and good humor takes a beating. He has little experience dealing with the level of criticism that he now endures, and as a result, he becomes irritable and depressed.

Meanwhile, Bill becomes more and more of a lame duck in the eyes of colleagues and subordinates as they see Henry's fingerprints on what should be Bill's work. He becomes a caricature of a business unit president. People start asking, "Why is Nick protecting Bill, anyway?"

Nick sits back in his chair and sighs. He hears the whispers of disapproval and bewilderment over his protection of Bill and a firestorm of complaints over Henry's performance and attitude. He knows he has to let Bill go, but now he wonders whether he'll be able to promote Henry to Bill's job. Given this mystifying downturn in his performance and the deterioration of his attitude, Henry is dropped from the list of potential successors to Nick.

Current Definition of Leadership

Our current definition of leadership works hand in glove with our prevailing governing values and with the absence of a more nuanced vocabulary for discussing responsibility to jointly perpetuate the Responsibility Virus.

We believe that when the chips are down, the leader should jump into the fray and take control, regardless of whether or not his or her capabilities are up to the task. At the slightest flinch from followers, we expect the leader to unilaterally assert control. We expect him or her to cover for subordinates by taking a wildly disproportionate share of the responsibility.

The leader as hero, which is reflected throughout our culture, is such a highly popular image because it has considerable appeal when times get tough. The captain who leaps to the helm. The doctor who saves a life in the emergency room. We write books and make movies about such people. We give them medals.

This mindset is based in part on the human tendency to adopt simple explanations for key events—explanations that rely on single causes.[1] We view the leader, if responsible, as *causally* responsible for an event. If there is only one cause, there is only one person who qualifies as the leader, by definition. Thus, the many nurses and assistants, engineers and scientists that have made the successful operating room experience possible see their contributions discounted in deference to the surgeon-as-leader model of the operation.

Henry's story is a case in point.

The boss called, Bill was in trouble, and it threatened the overall corporation. Bill needed help, and Henry leapt into the breach. He took charge as the heroic leader. This was no surprise. He had played this role before, saw himself as a natural for it, and felt comfortable leaping in.

And he did so in a particular way, a way that sought to protect his governing values. Henry sought *to win* by showing his boss and mentor, the man who would decide his next promotion, that he could bail him out while helping Bill, and while doing his own job, too. He sought *to maintain control* by carrying out his mission on his own, without so much as consultation from anyone else. Finally, he sought *to avoid embarrassment* and *stay rational* by not talking to Bill, lest the assignment embarrass the older man and cause some kind of outburst.

In fact, Henry was well into avoiding embarrassment when he didn't ask Nick at the very beginning why he was filling one of the three most important spots at WorldNet with an executive in whom he had almost no faith.

Had Henry engaged in a conversation with Bill, had he told him what his mission was, Bill might have asked Henry why he took the assignment without confronting Nick with its weak logic. Henry found it very convenient to be able to hold Bill, and his likely embarrassment in such a discussion, responsible for Henry's own failure in being forthright, when actually it was Henry's own embarrassment driving the choice not to be candid.

This illustrates another key, but implicit, feature of the current definition of leadership: the leader makes the unilateral seizing of responsibility undiscussable. Everybody knows the score. It's just that nobody feels comfortable talking about it. Nick doesn't, Bill doesn't, Henry doesn't, and other members of the WorldNet staff don't . . . except behind the backs of the key players.

The conspiracy of silence helps heroic leaders like Henry avoid embarrassment. They say to themselves: "Listen, I'm being a hero here. This is very challenging. And I'm doing it for others, not myself. I don't need the hassle of having all sorts of embarrassing conversations. I've got a job to do. I need to get on with it, not hold somebody's hand."

The conversation appears to make sense given our accepted definition of leadership, but it is not particularly true.

Henry is taking charge partly for his own benefit as well for the benefit of Nick and WorldNet. But revealing this self-serving aspect of his leadership would undermine its heroic image.

The heroic leader also bypasses conversations to avoid public testing of his actions. Again the implicit, internal logic is: "I'm being heroic. Everybody else is standing around acting helpless. This is a hard job. If I don't do it perfectly that's OK because I'm extending myself, being heroic. I'll be the judge of whether I've done a good job, not these sheep."

Once again, this implicit choice is designed to protect the governing values. In their own minds, leaders can award themselves a victory regardless of the outcome and thereby avoid the embarrassment of failure.

So "leadership" as Henry tried to exercise it involves four features:

1. splitting responsibility unilaterally,
2. seizing the disproportionate share,
3. making the seizing undiscussable, and
4. subjecting performance to private testing.

Current Definition of Followership

Our definition of followership is the mirror image of our flawed definition of leadership. Nobody gives medals to followers. Their wholly unromantic image is synonymous with passivity, getting out of the leader's way, and being led. To the extent that the leader is often seen as a hero, the follower is often characterized as a loser. This prejudice carries through consistently in structures ranging from social order in primates, to caste systems, dichotomies between aristocrats and peasants, free-wheeling cowpokes and slow-witted dirt farmers, and our own, more contemporary preference for risk takers and world shakers over those who "play it safe."

At WorldNet, even though he had managed to become head of a business unit, Bill was at heart a classic follower. He did not stand in the way of the unilateral split of responsibility made by Henry. In fact, he encouraged it by welcoming Henry's intervention. In the wake of Henry's heavily skewed division of their roles, Bill happily stepped aside, leaving Henry to struggle alone.

Bill also cooperated in making his abdication of responsibility undiscussable so as to avoid embarrassment—ostensibly Henry's embarrassment, but in reality his own. He did not discuss with Nick or anybody else Henry's increased role and his own decreased role. And, like Henry, he made his own performance in the diminished responsibilities subject to private, not public testing. That is, he convinced himself that only he knew his real responsibilities and therefore only he could be the judge.

In this entire range of followership behavior, Bill protected his governing values. He sought to win on the basis of performing a narrowed range of tasks and holding Henry responsible for shortcomings in the tasks he relinquished to him. Bill sought to maintain control by shrinking his responsibilities down to a territory he could control unilaterally. Finally, he sought to avoid embarrassment by making all of the above undiscussable.

Bill's followership illustrated the same four themes found in Henry's leadership:

1. allowing and/or encouraging the unilateral splitting of responsibility,
2. abdicating responsibility,

3. making the abdication undiscussable, and
4. subjecting performance to private testing.

Consequences of the Current Definitions

Despite all of these self-protective machinations, neither Henry nor Bill accomplished his goals, nor did Nick for that matter. Instead, as almost always happens, the Responsibility Virus got them, aided and abetted by the definitions of leadership and followership that shaped their actions.

No one was spared embarrassment. Instead, the Responsibility Virus produced a cornucopia of embarrassment, a hotbed of humiliation. Bill was mocked for becoming a shell of a former business unit president. Henry was mocked for trying to cover up the fact that he was doing Bill's job and for failing in his own. Even Nick suffered significant embarrassment for attempting to protect Bill and failing quite miserably in the attempt.

Both Bill and Henry lost big. Bill was fired, ending a long career in a most unsatisfying way. Henry was shifted to another role to "regain his momentum," which was more than enough to knock him off the CEO track.

By seeking to protect the governing values—which limited them to our current and highly flawed definitions of leadership and followership—they failed to protect anything. Ultimately, Bill and Henry both lost control of the situation. In due course, Nick had to step in and take charge, making decisions without so much as consulting either Henry or Bill. And they were not only casualties of their leadership and followership decisions, they produced significant collateral damage: Nick was pressured to step down and take early retirement in the wake of the debacle—a sad end to an otherwise spectacular career.

What all three needed was a productive reframing of leadership and followership. This is the same reframing we all need when we think about sharing responsibility.

A Redefinition of Leadership

The heroic definition of leadership aligned with images from books and movies leads directly to the Responsibility Virus. We need a new definition of leadership that inoculates us *against* the Responsibility Virus rather than contributing to it.

The first step is to see a leader not as one who makes unilateral and tacit decisions on the splitting of responsibility. Rather, leaders set their own responsibility and the responsibility of others through open dialogue. This is, of course, a tricky process and can easily lead to an infinite regress, as some measure of responsibility must be assumed for at least posing the question of responsibility in this way (and not in some other way) or for structuring the dialogue in one way rather than another.

Second, the redefinition should not see the leader as one who heroically takes charge, but rather as one who seeks to match capabilities and responsibilities for both self and others. A leader may indeed end up with a greater share of responsibility because of his or her greater capability, but not a share out of proportion with that capability. And with respect to any given matter, a leader may end up with a small share of responsibility because someone below can carry the weight, freeing the leader to work on other issues.

Third, in assuming responsibility, the redefined leader makes his or her reasoning explicit and invites contrary views on the appropriateness of the level chosen. Thus the apportionment of responsibility moves from the implicit and undiscussable to the open and very discussable. Finally,

---

FIGURE 10.1   Redefining Leadership

Current Definition	**Redefined Leadership**
• Split responsibility unilaterally	• Split responsibility through dialogue
• Seize disproportionate share of responsibility	• Apportion responsibilities in keeping with capabilities
• Make seizing of responsibility undiscussable	• Make apportionment discussable
• Subject performance to private testing	• Subject performance to public testing

---

in taking accountability for performance, leaders set standards that stretch but don't obviously outstrip capabilities, and make performance against those standards subject to public testing that extends well beyond the leader's own private assessment.

With respect to others, it is important for a leader to set responsibilities high so as to encourage growth. For the redefined leader, sharing responsibility is not a zero-sum game. Eliminating a leader's over-responsibility and the followers' under-responsibility enables both parties to test and build their skills, thereby advancing both their individual capabilities and the capabilities of their whole organization.

Regardless of how well we apportion responsibility, failure will happen, either because we erred in assigning responsibility, or because one of the parties did a bad job, or just because luck turned sour. In the traditional definition of leadership, the heroic leader jumps in at that point, takes charge, and fixes things. By contrast, the redefined leader jointly explores mutual responsibility for the failure, shares responsibility for the diagnosis, and works together to redesign the roles and responsibilities going forward.

What I am proposing could not be more different from current models of leadership.

Had Nick at WorldNet followed a redefined leadership model, he would not have gone behind Bill's back to Henry. Rather, he would have discussed his concerns about Bill's performance openly with Bill. He would have explored joint responsibility for the performance problems rather than tacitly blaming Bill and leaving it at that. Nick would have worked with Bill to design a new split of responsibilities that enabled Bill to perform a function consistent with his capabilities. Performance in this job could have been subject to public testing—that is, joint testing by both Nick and Bill. Likewise, corrective measures, to the extent that they were required, would have been jointly undertaken. One option might have been for Henry to play an explicit and public, rather than a clandestine, role in the corrective measures.

In this case, Nick was most responsible for spreading the Responsibility Virus by asking Henry to take the covert assignment. But Henry also was implicated in going along with Nick's ill-conceived plans. For his part, Bill fell prey to the downsides of unproductive followership. By unilaterally and tacitly stepping aside in deference to this ill-considered notion of leadership, Bill set himself up to be centrally implicated in the failures that resulted.

A Redefinition of Followership

Bill's role illustrates the need for us to redefine followership, as well. It would have been difficult for him to assert leadership or more productive followership in his situation—business problems, a boss who sends a fixer, and a fixer eager to start work—but he could have done more to resist the Virus.

A productive follower seeks to set his or her own level of responsibility not unilaterally but in conversation with the leader. In considering the appropriate level of responsibility, we make our reasoning explicit and invite contrary views. In accepting accountability for performance, we seek standards that stretch our capabilities, as well as public tests of performance.

Redefined followers seek to set high standards for responsibility in relation to the leader. This simultaneously discourages the leader's being over-responsible and encourages us to stretch and grow our own capabilities. At the critical point of failure, we do not unilaterally retreat, waiting for and implicitly encouraging the leader to take unilateral action. Rather, we seek to jointly explore mutual responsibility for the failure and jointly redesign the roles and responsibilities going forward.

We must hold the leader accountable for setting out his responsibility at a level consistent with capabilities. Somewhat paradoxically, we should hold the leader to a *higher standard* with respect to dialogue and cooperative design of responsibilities, while we simultaneously hold him to a *lower standard* with respect to the level of responsibility assumed. It is not our role to stand back and judge the leader, but rather to help and support him or her.

Just as for the leader, the key challenge for us is to learn to detect and override the entrenched governing values of *winning, maintaining control, avoiding embarrassment,* and *staying rational.*

By not retreating, and by choosing instead to step up to higher responsibility, we risk "losing," both in terms of failing

---

FIGURE 10.2   Redefining Followership

Current Definition	Redefined Followership
• Allow unilateral split of responsibility	• Split responsibility through dialogue
• Abdicate share of responsibility	• Apportion responsibilities in keeping with capabilities
• Make abdication of responsibility undiscussable	• Make apportionment discussable
• Subject performance to private testing	• Subject performance to public testing

---

at the task assigned and in not prevailing (that is, having the other's point of view win) in the discussions.

By determining our role and responsibilities through joint discussion, we give up total control and exchange it for the less comfortable joint control.

By opening up our performance to scrutiny, we create the possibility for observable failure and for the attendant embarrassment. Giving up these governing values is the toughest test of the redefined follower, as it is also for the redefined leader.

The current and redefined models of followership contrast as sharply as did those for leadership.

Had he been adhering to the redefined view of followership, Bill would have engaged Henry in a dialogue on the splitting of responsibilities. He would not have just passively accepted the split unilaterally and implicitly determined by

Henry. He would have contributed to the fashioning of a split of responsibilities that would have protected Henry from crashing and burning. By doing so, he also would have stretched himself. The discussion would have been open, which would have caused the resultant plan to be discussable more broadly in the organization. Finally, they could have kept on track through ongoing, joint, and open assessment, rather than private testing.

Summary Thoughts on Redefined Leadership/Followership

If you look back at the redefinitions of leadership and followership on the preceding pages, you will notice that they are identical, as shown in Figure 10.3.

In the old world, the definitions were in stark contrast—seizing responsibility versus abdicating responsibility—while in the redefined world they converge. Under this new definition, leaders and followers, in essence, have the same job—they are both dialogue partners, mutually responsible for the outcome. The only real difference is in the level of responsibility they take on coming out of the dialogue process. If the leader indeed has a higher level of relevant capabilities, he or she may end up taking on a higher level of responsibilities. However, the leader doesn't approach the task at hand with a fundamentally different frame.

Rather than making quick, tacit, and unilateral decisions, then going their separate ways, leaders and followers in this redefined world keep in closer contact and invest more in one another and in their joint understanding. The redefinitions, by inducing dialogue, understanding, and collaboration, reinforce themselves. As with the Responsibility Ladder, there are vicious downward—and virtuous upward—spirals, both very powerful.

When thinking about adopting these new definitions, there is little question that in the beginning redefined leadership will feel highly unleaderly for leaders, and redefined followership will feel downright scary for the followers. Both will entail learning to tolerate a higher level of personal discomfort.

In order to change behavior and embrace this discomfort, the redefined leader must keep up an internal conversation by constantly asking, "What have my previous leadership actions achieved?" Too often the answer will be failure, loss of control, and embarrassment. It held for Michael at the magazine, Jerry at GPC, Pierre at IDA, Willem at DevTek, Dwight at W&J, Carrie at SPI, Ned at STG, and Henry at WorldNet. It is the same story played over and over again. Flawed definitions of leadership designed to avert failure, maintain control, and avoid embarrassment invite the Responsibility Virus and with it, the very failure, loss of control, and embarrassment that we fear.

The redefined follower can ask the same question, "What have my previous followership actions achieved?" The answer for Caroline, Harry, Dick, Bill, and Hakeem is again: failure, loss of control, and embarrassment. On either side of the equation, in equal amounts, the traditional definitions simply don't work.

Reminders from this internal conversation will allow us to catch ourselves at the moment of truth, frame leadership and followership anew, carry out a modified course of action and, ideally, learn to embrace the collaboration, closeness, and positive energy that flows from these redefined roles.

It is worth noting that two of the most cherished leaders of the twentieth century, Winston Churchill and John F.

FIGURE 10.3   Redefining Leadership and Followership

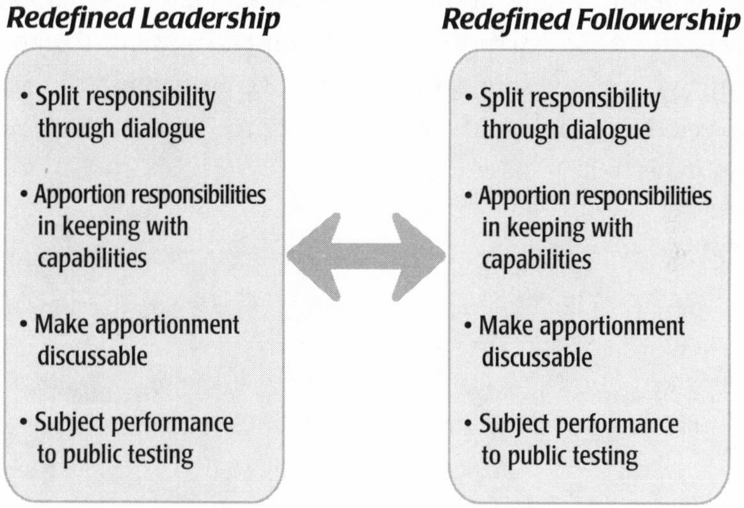

Redefined Leadership

- Split responsibility through dialogue

- Apportion responsibilities in keeping with capabilities

- Make apportionment discussable

- Subject performance to public testing

Redefined Followership

- Split responsibility through dialogue

- Apportion responsibilities in keeping with capabilities

- Make apportionment discussable

- Subject performance to public testing

Kennedy, are revered for asking their "followers" (that is, the citizens of their countries) to take responsibility, even more than they are revered for taking it on themselves. Churchill, promising blood, sweat, and tears, exhorted his country to hold firm and not give up during the darkest days of the Battle of Britain. "Let us brace ourselves to our duties and so bear ourselves that if the British Empire and its Commonwealth last for 1,000 years, men will still say: this was their finest hour." Kennedy's most memorable line was not a call for the government to take more responsibility. Rather, it was the admonition, "Ask not what your country can do for you; ask what you can do for your country."

In both cases, the call for greater responsibility on the part of the followers created a closer bond between the leader and his constituency, as well as a collective heightening of capabilities, resourcefulness, and engagement in the task at hand. Using traditional definitions from the "man on a horse" school of thought, they would have been classified as fundamentally unleaderly. However, through these collaborative actions, and with this more robust definition of leadership and followership, Churchill and Kennedy are both guaranteed their places in the pantheon of great leaders.

PART 4

Fighting the
Responsibility Virus

CHAPTER 11

Mired in
Under-Responsibility

Rick is a young accounting manager in the finance department of Simpson-Carr, a medium-sized auto parts company. Until about six months ago, part of his job had been managing the monthly closing of accounts. But he made some costly errors, and Shelley, the company controller, had quietly taken back the responsibility herself.

When Shelley first made the switch, Rick let out a big sigh of relief. Tabulating and balancing the results each month had been the most stressful thing he'd ever done. He felt bad about the mistakes, and he appreciated the way Shelley had made the shift without causing a big embarrassment. But now Rick has mixed feelings about that whole episode. He knows that Shelley already has her plate full and doesn't need another task. Watching from a safe distance, he realizes that he had been right on the verge of mastering the closings when Shelley took over the job. And he could do his new assignments in his sleep. As he thinks about the lack of challenge in what he's doing now, he gets that sinking feeling that he's taken a couple of serious steps backward.

But what's really starting to eat away at him is Shelley's attitude. Three or four times recently, when more interesting assignments came along, she gave them to the guy in the next cube. Shelley seems to see him as a "B-team" player now, one who is not a "go-getter" and never will be. And her attitude is rubbing off on everyone else. It's as if the whole office has begun to see him as the weak link. Certainly nobody comes to him for anything important.

"She's never outright demeaning or hostile," Rick thinks, "but Shelley has this sarcastic edge to her voice when she talks to me now. It's as if I've been assigned to her problem category, not her solutions category. I wish I could go into her office and take back the monthly closing job. But it's been six months and I've forgotten some of the procedures. I also don't know that I could take the mad scramble at the finish line each month. Not to mention the extra pressure. If I failed a second time, after asking for another chance, I'd be out on my ear. Maybe I'd better keep my mouth shut and do my job even if it is not particularly inspiring."

Rick is mired in a state of under-responsibility. It can happen with a boss, with friends, with teachers, or even with children. You know that you're doing less than you could. You know that you're losing the capacity to do things that you used to be able to do, and you certainly aren't moving your skills forward. People around you have started treating you as some sad case.

Taking on higher responsibility would demand consider-able initiative, but your lack of confidence makes that a scary thought. You don't like the feeling one bit, but you feel too conflicted about it to do anything but ride the gentle spiral downward.

Being stuck in this under-responsible state can be a seri-ous matter, and often a contributing factor in depression. Psychologists speak of this progressive inability to perform purposeful activities in an orderly fashion as "learned help-lessness."[1] It feeds on itself with increasingly negative self-assessments until you feel you'll be stuck forever in an un-pleasant, unsatisfying equilibrium. However, except in cases of extreme depression, you probably won't be.

The forces of static conservation of responsibility may drive you and your over-responsible partner (or partners) further and further from the balance point. You'll develop a hair-trigger in seeing passiveness/aggressiveness in the other. Like Rick, you'll see the slightest hint of aggressive behavior as a sign that you should back off still more. And your reaction will signal to the other person, as it did with Shelley, that they should seize a big-ger chunk of the responsibility from you. Because, after all, they have you pegged. You're under-responsible.

Eventually, this will produce a crash. The over-responsible party will falter under the weight and fail. The under-respon-sible person will get caught in the fallout of the overall failure even if he is convinced that he is not in any way at fault.

The crash can be quick or it can take a long time coming. When the crash takes a long time, the sense of being mired in under-responsibility can be wearying. And the longer the pe-riod until the crash, the greater the cost of the Virus. There is less collaboration, greater distancing between leaders and followers, greater misunderstanding and mistrust, greater at-rophy of skills.

As mentioned earlier, IBM went through such a slow, painful descent leading up to its crash in 1992–1993. The promise of lifetime employment by paternalistic leadership produced an environment of under-responsibility in the workforce that both contributed to the write-off and layoffs of 1992–1995 and left those laid off with fewer skills to build their post-IBM careers.

A Seven-Step Process for Escaping Under-Responsibility

How can people pull out of the downward spiral of under-responsibility before the crash? Feelings of inadequacy, depression, and learned helplessness, all too often reinforced by the over-responsible party, are factors that make it difficult. That's why escaping requires a series of baby steps, each of which is doable, each of which builds momentum and reinforces the courage to take the next step.

1) Visualize the End Result of the Path You're Traveling

Until the very end, the path of under-responsibility may be boring, but rarely is it so uncomfortable that it prompts someone to take decisive action. As in Rick's case, the absence of career momentum may feel disquieting, and the attitude of the over-responsible partner may be annoying, but one can get used to such feelings. Most insidiously, the memory of how it felt to be moving ahead, growing and stretching, begins to fade. Under-responsibility begins to feel not just inevitable but surprisingly normal. So without further reflection, it is hard to avoid the slow, steady drift.

That's why the first step in correcting the situation is to play out the steps that lie ahead. Imagine your over-responsible partner taking on incrementally more and more responsibility in the weeks and months ahead. Imagine yourself ceding responsibility at each and every turn. Imagine the resentment and animosity you and the partner will feel toward one another. Increasingly, the partner will see you as able to carry only a fraction of your true capacity. He or she will question your will and your character and will become more and more strident with you. You will come to question your own capabilities and character as you accept an ever-less-challenging life. Eventually, the over-responsible party will see you as dead wood that should be cut out. And even if they don't see you that way, after they succumb to failure and are replaced, their successor surely will.

Visualizing this worst-case scenario should help you muster the courage to take action. What reasonable course of action, no matter how miserably it fails, is going to make your situation worse? What could be worse than a passive and pointless descent into self-loathing and obsolescence? Clearly, you need to act.

2) Reframe the Over-Responsible Party

Following your visualization of the dismal future unless you make a change, turn your focus to the over-responsible party. At this point, they appear to you as overbearing, controlling, and cynical. In order to make them more approachable, you need to conduct a Frame Experiment in which you see them in a more productive light.

That reframing attempts to make sense out of what the partner has done. It's simplistic to see them as being overbearing, controlling, and cynical because that's simply the way they like to be. Few people actually enjoy exhibiting these negative qualities. It's far more likely that these traits and behaviors are a reaction to your behaviors, powered by static conservation of responsibility. As you've retreated, they've advanced. And as they've advanced into the vacuum you left, they've tried to make sense of your behavior. In the absence of open discussion, they've been forced to guess, and they've guessed that you are irresponsible or lazy or passive, or all of the above.

You need to see this other person as being just as trapped inside the static conservation of responsibility as are you. They are just as likely to feel helpless. Until the Virus is dealt with, they can't stop themselves from eating up ever more of your responsibilities and feeling ever more negative about you. They may be in a position of power, but they do not have the power to single-handedly reverse this tandem course that you're on.

Your existing frame probably looks like this:

Self: Helplessly mired in under-responsibility
Other: Overbearing, controlling, totally in charge
Task: Survive despite the unfortunate circumstances

Your new frame needs to look more like this:

Self: Mired in under-responsibility, but as capable as Other to get both out of it
Other: Stuck in over-responsibility, in part because of Self; feeling helpless to change anything; not happy with own actions/attitude
Task: Attempt to work with Other to start toward a more productive sharing of responsibilities

With this revised Frame in your head, you're now ready to have a productive conversation with your over-responsible counterpart.

3) Pick a Burning Issue on Which You Want to Work

Think about the issues of under-responsibility that bother you most. Choose one that really bugs you, but not the one that's most difficult to redress. For example, Rick shouldn't pick the issue of regaining responsibility for the monthly closing. That's simply too great a leap. But how could Rick judge which steps are too high and which are appropriate?

One key indicator is whether or not he can maintain a positive reframe as he imagines tackling the issue with the over-responsible party. If he can't, then he should pick a simpler issue. In Rick's case, it might be Shelley's apparent propensity to overlook him as she hands out new tasks within the department. There may be less emotion, less pain, and fewer negative attributions associated with this issue, and freedom from that baggage improves the odds for success.

The goal is simply to arrest the downward spiral that leaves you mired in under-responsibility, not eliminate the under-responsibility in one fell swoop.

4) Engage in a Responsibility Ladder Conversation

Equipped with the Frame Experiment, engage your over-responsible counterpart in a conversation, the goal of which is to mutually agree on your taking a higher level and their taking a lower level of responsibility on your issue of choice. For this you need the Responsibility Ladder to structure the conversation.

Begin by indicating that you feel that you are not taking as much responsibility as you can or should and that you would like to remedy it. Provide examples of situations in which you could have taken on more.

Rick could say to Shelley: *"Ever since I made the errors on the monthly closing and stopped doing that, I've found myself shrinking back from taking on tasks. You asked for volunteers for a receivable reconciliation and I didn't come forward. In several other cases, you've given work to others, and I haven't offered to help them, even though I had the experience and training necessary."*

Continue by describing your understanding of the status quo. Even though it is not optimal or productive, it does make sense that both you and the other have developed an increasingly pessimistic view of your capabilities. Your actions have, so far, encouraged and validated those negative assumptions. Because these assessments are sensible, they are likely to continue unless you both choose to break out of the downward spiral.

Rick could say: *"I can understand how this is happening. I don't have much confidence, and I probably don't signal much that's positive to you. I probably make you nervous about giving me more tasks, so you take them on yourself or hand them to someone else. So neither of us is inclined at any particular moment to do something that changes this dynamic."*

It's important not to blame the other person disproportionately for the current state of affairs. First, that characterization is probably dead wrong—remember it takes two to tango. Second, it will appear to the over-responsible party to be further proof that you are under-responsible if you don't shoulder a fair share of the blame. And third, it will probably aggravate the other party, causing them to take a less productive approach to the conversation and your effort to rise out of under-responsibility.

Next, you indicate your desire to change the dynamic for your mutual benefit, and ask for their help in doing so. Describe the ways in which the dynamic is hurting both you (your skills are atrophying, you're not growing, your confidence is waning) and the other (she's overburdened). Assert that you are willing to help, but will need her help as well.

Rick could say: *"This isn't good for me. I don't think I'm becoming more skilled. In fact, I think just the opposite is happening. I'm getting complacent and unconfident. And you have to deal with much more than you should. You either take on work of mine that you shouldn't have to, or you have to worry about figuring out who else in the office should do it. I want to take on more to help myself and to help you, but to do so I'm going to need your support and cooperation."*

The next part of the conversation should suggest using the Responsibility Ladder to rebuild your level of responsibility. You should pick a task on which you are operating at a lower rung on the ladder than you think you could, and suggest taking on an incrementally higher level of responsibility.

Rick could say: *"You know how I process the credit requests from sales? Whenever they're within our standard limits, I approve them myself and just fill out the forms. When they're above the limits, I always bring them to you and ask you what to do. I never get any better and you always have to do all the thinking. Why don't I start coming to you with my analysis of the customer, my thinking on the request, and my recommendation? You could then tell me what you think of my analysis and recommendation and either confirm it or make a different decision. If you make a different decision, you can tell me in what ways my thinking was flawed and I can learn. Over time I hope I'll learn enough to be able to minimize or eliminate entirely the time you need to spend on credit requests."*

5) Use the Choice Structuring Tool to Gain Comfort

You can use aspects of the Choice Structuring Tool to explore whether both parties are comfortable with, or can be made comfortable with, the enhanced division of responsibilities and to assess performance on the new responsibilities going forward. In particular, the parties can use it to explore the thinking behind their positions. They can both ask the question: What would you have to believe for the new split of responsibilities to be appropriate from the perspective of both parties? If one or the other has distinct reservations about certain conditions, those reservations can be subjected to testing and the new split of responsibilities can be confirmed or rejected.

In this regard, Rick and Shelley could both reflect on what they would have to believe about one another for Rick's suggestion to make sense. For example, Shelley would have to believe that Rick has enough skill to come up with credit recommendations good enough to warrant her consideration. And she would have to believe that Rick would actually be able to learn from her feedback, making it worth her time to hear his reasoning and provide coaching. Rick would have to believe the same thing as Shelley's first condition, that is, that he has enough skill to produce recommendations that warrant her consideration. In addition, he would have to believe that Shelley would be willing and able to provide sufficient feedback on his reasoning and recommendations for him to actually learn and perfect his skills in this area.

Were they to come to the conclusion that they each believed their two conditions to hold, they could move forward confidently on the new split of responsibility. However, if they harbored some doubts as to whether certain conditions held, they could jointly design tests to help overcome their doubts.

Let's assume that Shelley doubted her second condition (that is, that Rick would learn from her feedback, making it worth her time), and that Rick doubted his second condition (that Shelley would be willing to provide sufficient feedback for him to learn). They may well come to the conclusion that they can't predict with certainty, and that the only way to find out is to run a controlled experiment for a month. In the experiment, Shelley will commit to providing feedback and they will assess Rick's advancement to see whether it suggests the likelihood of further advancement. Ultimately, Shelley would assess whether the expenditure of her time is worth the positive outcome.

It's important in designing the test to make the results subject to public testing between the two of them, not private testing within the mind of either. If the testing stays private, other parties never understand why they've failed (or passed, for that matter). That keeps them from learning. So Shelley would need to commit to explaining why she came to her conclusion at the end of the month, and Rick would have to do the same. Only then would they both really understand whether the premise of Rick increasing his responsibility level is valid or not.

6) Do It and Reflect

At this point, the job is to do it and reflect on performance and learning. By "do it," I mean start to carry out the higher level of responsibilities. This may feel frightening at first, but the first five steps of this process are designed, in part, to minimize the fear as much as possible. The stakes are far lower when compared to the dismal prospects that would follow from doing nothing, and the focus is on taking only a baby step. And the over-responsible partner is committed to collaborate on reversing the downward spiral. All of which is designed to make it easier for the under-responsible individual to start taking actions that change course.

Equally important, you need to reflect on your own performance as you take on the new level of responsibility. Assess your own performance against the criteria set up in advance and test your assessment with the other party. By testing openly, you give the other party confidence that you are receptive to feedback. This helps them recognize that they don't have to resort to private tests and private fixes when things go wrong. Instead, they can have a timely conversation with you that can lead to fine adjustments in responsibility rather than extreme and unproductive shifts.

The dialogue also builds confidence in the two parties that they can work together and collaborate. By taking the initiative, the under-responsible party begins to convince the over-responsible party that he or she doesn't have to keep taking on too much to make up for the deficit of the under-responsible party.

In addition, they signal to one another the intent to engage in an ongoing dialogue that helps fine-tune responsibility levels between themselves going forward. This will foster a sense of closeness and collaboration between the two, replacing the gulf that was building between them. This collaborative approach will continuously pull them toward the appropriate balance point between capabilities and responsibilities and not let them drift away.

7) Repeat the Above Six Steps Over and Over

The final step is to repeat the above six steps over and over until you no longer feel mired in under-responsibility. This may mean repeating the steps with the same person on a more difficult issue or with a different person in a different context where you also feel you've been under-responsible. The hope is that the initial baby step out of the mire will give you sufficient confidence to take another step and another and another.

Rick, buoyed by his success in dealing with the credit approval issue, may now wish to tackle the trickier issue of the monthly closings. Perhaps he may feel comfortable approaching Shelley about it. On the other hand, he may still feel caught in under-responsibility generally, and he may need to follow the process with another person, either at work or in another part of his life.

For the person truly mired in under-responsibility, working on one issue with one person won't necessarily eliminate the feeling and eradicate the problem. It will, however, arrest the downward spiral and provide the confidence necessary to repeat the process until the person has better matched responsibilities to capabilities.

CHAPTER 12

Trapped in
Over-Responsibility

Floyd sits in the office of Maplebrook Mills, the agribusiness firm he founded twenty-seven years ago. It is still what commentators referred to as a small business, with $30 million in sales. But Floyd is rightly proud of its strong competitive position against many larger firms.

At this very instant, however, Floyd is a tired and somewhat discouraged man. He is in on a Saturday afternoon, trying to unravel the mess created by his VP of sales. Hal is a stereotypical sales guy, eager to please, and he has been far too loose with credit policy over the last six months. On Friday, the bank called worried about the ballooning size of the customer receivables, as well as the increased bank debt Maplebrook required to finance them.

"Floyd," the bank manager said, "we're feeling a wee bit nervous about your operating line. Are you sure everything's all right over there, or do we need to sit down and talk?"

Floyd was more embarrassed than nervous about the call. The bank manager was a good friend and not inclined toward aggressive action. However, he wished that Art, Maplebrook's CFO, had given him a heads up. Floyd had resolved to follow the receivables increase and the loan balance more closely going forward. Art didn't seem to have the sense to keep him informed of the right stuff. However, it was the conversation with Hal on Friday afternoon that had gotten under his skin. When he asked Hal about the receivables situation, Hal had just shrugged his shoulders as if to say, "Hey, I'm on the hook to sell a lot of product. If I have to overextend a bit on credit to make the sales, what can I do?"

That was the moment when it finally dawned on Floyd that Hal was never, ever going to mature into being his successor. Hal knew how to sell, but he couldn't manage his way out of a paper bag. He never wanted to be bothered by the wider business issues, like whether the people he was selling to could pay, and whether the sales were ever going to mean a profit for Maplebrook. As far as Hal was concerned, that was Floyd's job.

"I've got to manage to the profitability of the business," Floyd muttered to himself as he flipped through the printouts, "because Hal can't or won't think about anything but sales. And I've got to manage the relationship with the bank because Art wants to stick to the internal financial world and doesn't like all the nasty complications of the external world. And I have pretty much got to oversee logistics and purchasing, too, because our guys only understand the basics, not the strategy behind it. I'm fifty-three, and my plan to be largely out of the day-to-day management of the firm by fifty-five is a total pipe dream. And truth be told, I'm tired of this place. My back gets sore and I would truly rather be golfing. I feel a little silly, the only guy putting in time Saturdays who isn't getting paid by the hour."

For every person who feels mired in under-responsibility there is probably someone who feels trapped in and burdened by over-responsibility. Sometimes it means taking on harder tasks than you're capable of handling, but more often it means loading yourself up with everyone else's work until, like the proverbial camel, you collapse under the weight. You know that people see you as overbearing, aggressive, and demanding. They are disinclined to take the initiative because they think it's redundant—you'll do the job anyway—and you'd probably criticize their way of doing it. And you don't really trust them in any case, because you haven't seen any signs that they're able to step up to the plate. You feel trapped, but also conflicted. This leaves you stuck spiraling upward in responsibility and downward in satisfaction.

But take heart. Except in rare cases in which power and responsibility become an obsession and one's only source of value, the forces of static conservation of responsibility sooner or later will break the deadlock. They will drive you and your under-responsible partner (or partners) farther and farther from the balance point. Both of you will develop a hair-trigger on seeing passiveness/aggressiveness in the other. Like Floyd, you will see the slightest hint of passive behavior as a sign that you should take charge more. And your reaction will signal to the other people, like Hal and Art, that they should back down farther. As we've seen so many times before, the pattern will, in time, produce a crash when the over-responsible party swoons under the weight and fails.

At IBM, while rank-and-file employees became increasingly under-responsible for their own and their firm's success, the executives were forced to take on an ever higher level of responsibility. This burden, on top of an implicit and conflicting commitment to increase shareholder value, was too much of a strain for the executives to bear and IBM crashed spectacularly. At the point of the crash in 1992, the managers executed a classic flip of responsibility and blamed the complacent employees, the stock market, and unfair competition, rather than their own choices and behaviors in supporting an unworkable system of lifetime employment guarantees.

A Process for Escaping Over-Responsibility

How can people trapped in over-responsibility escape before the eventual crash? That may be an even trickier question than for the under-responsible person. The over-responsible person is, if anything, more oblivious to the downsides of their stance. They feel invincible, able to take on their job and the jobs of others. They have firmly planted in their minds the traditional definition of the heroic leader, and they are playing it to the hilt. While those mired in under-responsibility feel a strong sense of shame at being in a position that is widely denigrated, those trapped in over-responsibility feel a sense of nobility, as well as noblesse oblige.

A similar set of steps can be used to escape over-responsibility.

1) *Visualize the End Result of the Path You're Traveling*

Until the very end, the over-responsible person feels capable of overcoming all presenting challenges so is disinclined to change. They err on the side of over-responsibility precisely because they think that they are more capable than anyone else. And the behavior of others in the face of their over-responsibility reinforces the belief that they are the only one who can save the day. Floyd may feel tired and overworked, but he's sure Hal and Art can't be trusted with the task at hand, so he sees little choice but to bear down and work harder. He gets used to carrying a disproportionate weight and forgets what it's like to do anything less. Hal and Art watch him devour responsibility and they back off, prompting Floyd to seize more, and so on. Without further reflection, it is hard to avoid the slow, steady drift into extremes caused by the push of static conservation of responsibility.

The first step, once again, is to visualize the logical extension of this behavior. Play out the steps well into the future. Imagine your under-responsible partner(s) taking on incrementally less and less. Imagine yourself seizing more responsibility at each and every turn. Imagine the psychological toll as you and your partner(s) develop increasing contempt for one another. You will see them as increasingly pathetic and they will see you as increasingly domineering.

Get concrete. Focus on the increase in workload that you will be forced to bear. Look at all the tasks you've taken on as you've declared your partner(s) to be incapable or incompetent. Add up these tasks and identify the time period over which you've assumed them—say the past three years. Construct in your mind an equal number of added tasks/responsibilities to be added over the next three years. Visualize what your life will be like in another three years with these additional tasks stacked on top of the current load. Then imagine another three years and another load, and then another three.

If you can visualize the load as being heavier than any one person can bear, even someone with your impressive skills and capacity, you will become motivated to consider an alternative scenario. You will recognize that, whatever the danger you associate with trying to redistribute the burden with under-responsible partners in whom you have little trust, it pales beside the danger of the path you see before you otherwise.

2) Reframe the Under-Responsible Party

Following the visualization, turn your focus to the under-re-sponsible party(parties). At this point, the parties appear weak, pathetic, and perhaps lazy. In order to convert them into partners you can see worthy of responsibility, you must conduct a Frame Experiment in which you cast them in a more productive light. Right now Hal and Art seem so lim-ited and helpless to Floyd that he could never shift meaning-ful responsibilities to them, even if he had visualized, and feared, the long-term consequences of his over-responsibility.

Again, the way to reframe them is to make sense out of their pattern of actions. They are unlikely to be pathetic and weak because they love being pathetic and weak. In fact, they have their strengths. Hal has fabulous selling skills. Put him head-to-head against the lead salesmen of competitors and he wins hands down. A more sensible explanation for his pathetic and weak attitude and behavior is as a reaction to your behaviors, powered by static conservation. As you advanced, the others retreated. And as they retreat and you advance, they try to make sense out of your behavior, which leads them to guess that you are overbearing, domineering, and untrusting.

The static conservation of responsibility has trapped all of you in your fixed positions of seizing and ceding responsibility.

The Frame Experiment to help you see this is the mirror image of the one in the last chapter. It would start with the existing frame, which would look approximately like this:

Self: Burdened by and trapped in over-responsibility
Other: Weak, pathetic, requiring me to carry them
Task: Soldier on heroically

The new frame would look approximately like this:

Self: Trapped in over-responsibility in substantial part
of my own making
Other: Mired in under-responsibility, in part because
of Self; feeling helpless to change anything; not
happy with own actions/attitude
Task: Attempt to work with Other to start toward a
more productive sharing of responsibilities

This is a far better frame for conducting a more productive conversation with your under-responsible counterpart(s).

3) Pick a Burning Issue on Which You Want to Work

As with the process for under-responsibility, choose an issue of over-responsibility that is bugging you, but not the toughest one. This is a more difficult issue for the over-responsible hero, who tends to go directly toward the toughest issue simply because the challenge seems most heroic. Floyd would be inclined to pick the issue of Hal's not taking responsibility for the profitability of the business overall. That is a very broad, complex, and abstract issue. The better choice would Hal's performance on managing customer credit risk. If Hal were to do a better job at that, Floyd might feel more willing to hand him incrementally more responsibility for managing profitability in other ways—for example, in taking over pricing policy.

So the advice here is to resist being over-responsible in picking an issue to begin tackling over-responsibility. Pick an issue that gives the under-responsible party(parties) a chance to prove that they can and will help you overcome your self-defeating tendencies.

Floyd needs to determine whether he can maintain a positive reframe for an encounter with Hal or Art to tackle the issue in question. If he can't maintain a positive frame, then he can pick an easier issue with less emotion, less pain, and fewer negative attributions. The goal is to arrest the spiral that leaves you trapped in over-responsibility, not eliminate the over-responsibility in one fell swoop. Getting a good start to build momentum is the critical thing.

4) Engage in a Responsibility Ladder Conversation

Equipped with the Frame Experiment, you can engage your under-responsible counterpart in a conversation, the goal of which is to mutually agree on a redistribution of responsibility on your issue of choice. The Responsibility Ladder is the tool you can use to structure the conversation.

Begin the conversation by indicating that you feel that you're seizing too much responsibility and that is not helpful to your colleagues or you. It is critical to avoid making others feel blamed for the current state. Very likely, they already feel uncomfortable about their under-responsibility. If you trigger further feelings of embarrassment at the start of this conversation, the others are likely to engage in evasive action to protect their governing values. Throughout the conversation, start with descriptions of your over-responsibility. Make clear that you are sharing responsibility for the problem.

Provide examples to illustrate ways in which you have jumped too quickly in taking on responsibility in situations where you could have left more of it in their hands.

Floyd could say to Hal: *"Three years ago our pricing got out of line, and we sold part of the product line below cost, and ever since I've taken over complete control of pricing. I just did it myself on Saturday afternoons and handed it to you and the salespeople without any explanation. By doing it all behind closed doors, I didn't give you any chance to learn how I think about pricing and practice. I think that's been an error on my part."*

Continue by describing the way in which this situation makes sense, even though not optimal or productive.

Floyd could say: *"I can understand why it stays this way. I haven't given you any indication that I want your help, and I haven't given you any insight into how I price. And I'm the CEO. I'm not a bit surprised that you've simply accepted my decision on allocation of this assignment and focused on doing your other work. On Saturday afternoons I sometimes think: Why doesn't Hal do this? But it's completely understandable that you don't. Nor is it likely that anything whatsoever is going to change."*

It's important to share the blame for the current state of affairs. The under-responsible party will be highly sensitive to being blamed for something they're powerless to change, whether that feeling is well grounded or not.

Next indicate your desire to change the dynamic for everyone's sake. Make it very clear that you need their help in doing so. Describe the way in which the dynamic is hurting you both, starting with you but including them.

Floyd could say: *"This is not good for me. I'm feeling overworked and the firm is becoming too dependent on me, which is not in its long-term interests. I'm getting tired and overworked while you're getting rusty. I'd like to work with you to provide more opportunities for you to assume responsibilities, and I'd like your assistance in helping me take on less. I've fallen into bad habits on that front, and I'll need you to alert me when I grab responsibility that I shouldn't."*

You can then use the Responsibility Ladder to design a way for you to start your downward migration in responsibility. You should pick a task on which you're operating at too high a rung on the ladder and the other person too low, and suggest balancing the responsibility.

Floyd could say: *"Currently I set all the credit limits for all the customers, Hal, and just give you the final results. But you know the customers as well as or better than I do. Why don't you take a crack at setting preliminary limits? You can show me your analysis and results and I'll give you my feedback. If I make any changes, I'll give you my reasoning so you'll have that knowledge for the next time. When we get to the point of my accepting the vast majority of your recommendations, I can turn over the credit setting to you entirely. I think that would be better for you, better for me, and better for Maplebrook."*

5) Use the Choice Structuring Tool to Gain Comfort

Again, you can use the Choice Structuring Tool to become comfortable with the new division of responsibilities and to assess performance on the new responsibilities by exploring the underlying assumptions. As before, the key question is: What would we have to believe for the new split of responsibilities to be appropriate from the perspective of both parties?

Floyd and Hal could reflect on what they would have to believe about one another for Floyd's suggestion to make sense. For example, Floyd would have to believe that Hal has enough skill to come up with credit recommendations that make sense for the business as a whole, not just from Hal's narrow sales perspective. He also would have to believe that Hal would take his feedback to heart and learn from it. Hal would have to believe he would be able to provide a useful set of recommendations, not ones that Floyd would just reject out of hand, and that Floyd would actually take the time to provide feedback. Hal also would have to believe that he was capable of learning and moving ahead as suggested by the plan.

Were they to come to the conclusion that they each believed their conditions to hold, they could move forward confidently on the new split of responsibility. However, if they harbored any doubts, they could jointly design tests to help overcome those doubts. Floyd and Hal could choose to run a controlled experiment, as Shelley and Rick did. Or alternatively, they could agree that Hal should take a credit analysis course at the local business school before starting the plan. Or they could agree that Floyd needs some counseling in giving useful feedback before they try the plan.

If they run the controlled test, or Hal takes a course or Floyd takes counseling, they need to make the results of these tests subject to the joint assessment of the two, not subject only to private testing within the mind of either. So if Floyd takes a couple of counseling sessions on giving feedback and declares himself to be set without checking with Hal (or his counselor), he will not provide Hal with the confidence that the new division of responsibilities will work. And if he lacks the confidence, he will probably back off and shrink back to a lower level of responsibility as soon as possible.

In order for the under-responsible member of the pair to take what would feel to be a risky and dangerous step upward in responsibility, the over-responsible member has to recognize the fear and ensure that they are modeling a more productive behavior with their actions. In particular, they need to make their reasoning very clear, using the Choice Structuring Process, and to make their actions open to public testing and critique. If the over-responsible party doesn't do so, it is very unlikely that the under-responsible party will do so. And that is likely to thwart any forward progress.

6) Do It and Reflect

In letting go a bit, the over-responsible partner will feel some level of fear that he's courting failure. But the under-responsible party will feel as much fear or more. It's important for the over-responsible members to avoid hovering like a vulture, waiting for the first chance to swoop in and grab back the responsibility they've surrendered. If they do, the under-responsible parties will question the commitment of the Other to change their behavior. So it is important for Floyd to give Hal time and space to work on the recommendations and to come forward when he is ready.

Each partner needs to reflect on his own performance as he takes on the new level of responsibility. Floyd needs to ask himself: Did I give Hal encouragement and latitude to come up with a set of credit recommendations? Did I give him helpful feedback where I felt uncomfortable with his recommendations? Where he made mistakes, did I provide counsel to him and give him a second chance, or did I seize back responsibility right away? More important, he needs to ask those questions of Hal so that the answers are not just self-serving affirmations but answers that give insight into his impact on

Hal. Hal's feedback will enable Floyd to take corrective actions in his own behavior if warranted. Floyd also can give useful feedback to Hal on his behavior. Did Hal shrink back to lower responsibility as soon as the going got tough, or did he hang in there in a way that suggested his seriousness about stepping up to a higher level of responsibility?

This dialogue will build confidence in both parties that they can communicate with each other. By taking the initiative, Floyd convinces Hal that he doesn't want to be overbearing and controlling, but rather needs Hal's help to overcome his most over-responsible tendencies. But he also needs to make it clear that this is a collaboration requiring that Hal step up to a greater level of responsibility. As he does so, Hal increases Floyd's confidence that he will not have to keep taking on more and more responsibility, even as he gets older and would prefer to be planning his retirement. They begin to see each other as part of the solution, not part of the problem. This will build a sense of closeness and collaboration, which itself will provide a resistance against the Responsibility Virus.

7) Repeat the Above Six Steps Over and Over

The final step is to repeat the previous six steps over and over until you no longer feel trapped in over-responsibility. For Floyd this means both tackling bigger issues with Hal, such as managing firm profitability overall, while starting to tackle issues with Art and other members of his management team. With each successive issue successfully addressed, Floyd will feel less and less trapped in an uncomfortable world of over-responsibility. In due course, he may feel that he has achieved a balance in which he does not see himself heading toward a crash.

Working on one small issue of over-responsibility will not eradicate the Responsibility Virus, but the hope is that the results of the initial baby step out of the trap will give you sufficient confidence to pursue another step and another and another. At a minimum, it will arrest the downward spiral, which in turn should provide the confidence necessary to repeat the process until you have matched responsibilities to capabilities in your life.

CHAPTER 13

The Challenge
Facing Professionals

While everyone is prone to infection, the professional represents the Typhoid Mary of the Responsibility Virus, and professional relationships the fertile environment for transmission. To truly help their clients, professionals must learn to inoculate themselves and their practices against the disease. Otherwise, they will spend much of their professional lives spreading rather than helping to control it.

There are, of course, innumerable classifications of professionals. Many are in the health sciences, including doctors, nurses, dentists, and chiropractors, as well as psychologists and therapists of various persuasions. Then there are lawyers, engineers, consultants, actuaries, architects, educators, athletes, and so on.

Despite their diversity, these people share a common *relationship structure* and it consistently gets them into trouble.

Professionals are by definition expert service providers. Their capacity to provide the service in question is based both on specific education—which is typically challenging and complicated—and years of practice in their field, often including apprenticeship in some form mandated by their professional licensing body. Professionals accordingly see themselves as uniquely qualified in their field and we seek signals of that expertise when we hire them. By hiring them we send them a signal that we think that they indeed are uniquely capable. In fact, professional groups seek to establish jurisdiction over particular problems and phenomena, as articulated by sociologist Andrew Abbott.[1] Psychiatrists, for instance, establish jurisdiction over problems such as hyperactivity, depression, and explosive behavior by first labeling them and then showing how the empirical body of evidence on which psychiatry rests is relevant to the now-labeled problem, and finally by assuming professional responsibility for advice relating to the problem. Professional responsibility—and the profits that accrue—is the reward for being able to successfully establish jurisdiction—to become a monopolist over expertise in that field.

We seek professionals' services because we have a problem or shortcoming in a domain in which we are not expert and we believe that they are. I went to my doctor when my ears hurt for a month and I got worried. I went to an architect when I wanted to build a cottage that would pass building codes, look attractive, and meet my family's needs. The last time I went to my lawyer was when I needed to update my will. The very act of seeking professional help signals to the professional and ourselves that we know we are incapable of solving our own problems. Thus, the Responsibility Virus dynamic begins building even as we make the appointment.

In reality and in perception, we think (and signal) that they are capable in this domain and that we are not. This capability gap is enhanced by the language system that professionals use—which makes their expertise inscrutable to lay criticism and opinion.[2]

In most cases, we see it as a big step to hire a professional, so we tend to do so only if the issue in question is important—that is, there is potential for a big downside or big upside—and it is so complex that we are incapable of resolving it ourselves. The very large costs of seeking professional advice—costs often directly borne by the seeker of the advice—mean that going to visit a professional sets up an environment in which we may be quite willing to abdicate responsibility for any form of partnership in addressing the problem at hand. Studies show that once we pay for professional services, we resolve the cognitive dissonance between "This advice costs a lot" and "This advice may be potentially useless and even harmful" with an explanation such as "This advice must actually be very valuable, which is to say, valid."

We tend to pay a handsome sum for the service both because it is an important issue and because the professional values their time highly (typically because they can).

Professionals by and large understand the nature of this structure very well. In fact, I would argue that they are attracted to a professional field by this very structure. In this structure, they get to play the role of the expert who is in control of the situation. Professionals tend to be people who like achieving a level of expertise that sets them apart from their fellow man. They also get to play the role of a helper to the client. So they can be both expert and altruist at the same time, while, if they are good, getting paid handsomely for their troubles.

From the outset, this relationship structure generates substantial fear of failure in both client and professional. The client experiences helplessness and fear that the professional help may not be able to produce a successful outcome. Ironically, the client knows that the reason that he's hiring the professional is that, as a layman, he doesn't know enough about the matter at hand. But for the very reason that he doesn't know much about the matter at hand, he realizes that he is incapable of judging for certain the professional's actual capabilities. The jargon in which professional expertise is cloaked certainly does not make these judgments any easier. If we knew enough to judge for certain, we would know enough about the matter at hand that we wouldn't have to hire the professional in the first place. In this, the logic is circular. You either know enough and don't need a professional or you don't know enough and have to guess at the professional's true qualifications.

The professional experiences fear at the outset that the task at hand may be so difficult that he or she may struggle or even fail. In part this is because at the outset the task that the professional agrees to accept is ill defined. The client, who doesn't have the specific or the general knowledge possessed by the professional, struggles to explain what he or she needs, so the professional must guess at the nature and scope of the task.

When I phone up my doctor and say "I have a pain in my side so I need to see you," my doctor has very little way of knowing the complexity of the assignment. It may be indigestion, appendicitis, or liver cancer—very different problems. When a CEO hires a strategy consultant to fix his business problem, the strategy consultant won't know how difficult the task will be until weeks or months on the job. After all, if the CEO could actually identify the problem, he probably would solve it himself rather than hire the consultant.

So at this initial stage, with both parties experiencing considerable apprehension, the professional—who has become a professional in part because he or she likes to be in control—reads the client's first sign of discomfort as justification for leaping into the saddle and engaging in traditional leadership behavior. To guard against losing, to maintain control, to avoid embarrassment, and to stay rational, the professional seizes responsibility unilaterally and starts to work. The clients, already feeling vulnerable and incapable, tend to stand back and watch, lapsing into traditional followership behavior. They have already tried to maintain control by hiring a professional to exert control on their behalf. Now they will win by holding the professional responsible, and avoid embarrassment by not revealing their underlying fears.

With that very first characteristic move, the Responsibility Virus gets a powerful start and never looks back. The client's passivity convinces the professional that he or she has been right to seize control. The professional's aggressiveness convinces the client that he or she has been right to step aside. By that point, any balance in the relationship structure is difficult to retrieve. The professional and client distance themselves from one another, with the professional earning his fee by taking on the lion's share of the choice-making responsibility.

Since the problems that bring professional and client together are often short-lived (though not always—the relationship between a client and therapist, for instance, may last for many years), the result of the Virus is not always outright failure. Static conservation of responsibility doesn't push the imbalance that far.

However, the Virus profoundly limits the benefits of the engagement. This sub-optimization stems from the degree to which the client's capabilities and insights are simply not brought to bear in the relationship structure, and in the business at hand. Another unfortunate consequence is that the relationship is far less emotionally satisfying to the client.

We all have experienced the frustration of dealing with a classic take-charge doctor. I once nervously rushed to the hospital with my daughter, who had fallen off a horse and, as it turned out, broken her elbow. The doctor asked very few questions, listened little if at all to my fears and concerns or to my description of the fall, and made 100 percent of the choices with the minimal amount of consultation considered acceptable by the profession (and quite possibly the courts). He concluded at the outset that I could contribute little, and used me as a data source only when absolutely necessary. Clearly he did not see me as a partner in reaching the best medical solution.

Not unexpectedly, we got a bad result. In our case, he diagnosed the break as the kind one gets from over-stressing the arm trying to brace oneself from a fall, palm first with the arm extended straight, which happens in 90 percent of elbow breaks. But in the other 10 percent of cases, including my daughter's, the elbow bone is shattered by landing directly on its underside with the arm bent and palm never striking the ground. He made the diagnosis despite my attempt to show him exactly how my daughter fell. The result was that the doctor put on the cast inappropriately, which meant that it pulled the broken bones apart rather than held them together.

This experience was painful for my daughter and highly alienating for both of us. I felt that the doctor neglected to consider my viewpoint, even though I had something important to contribute. I came away feeling that my daughter was the victim of unilateral choices. Only when we switched to a doctor whom I knew well and who listened carefully to our story and recognized that he was dealing with the 10 percent case rather than the 90 percent case did my daughter get on the road to recovery.

When the choices are obviously bad and the outcome problematic or disastrous, take-charge doctors, while feeling genuine remorse, see themselves as having tried heroically to do the best job they could under the circumstances. They feel themselves as either the victim of bad luck or of an impossible situation. They are blind to the degree of empowerment they could have gained by listening to and collaborating with the client in a more productive fashion.

Given the traditional structure of these relationships, however, the blindness is not surprising. The patient takes the doctor's signal at the outset and disappears from decisionmaking sight, lowering to zero the doctor's expectations of useful collaboration.

Alternatively, many of us have hired what turns out to be the imperialistic architect who listens to us as little as possible and designs the house that he/she would like to live in rather than a house that suits our needs. Or we hire a combative lawyer who gets into fights with the other side over points of law in which we have no interest. Or we hire a consultant who brings in a team that races off to solve what it thinks is our problem, without ever verifying our viewpoint, or whether the solution being built is even relevant to our needs.

Because of the relationship structure, many professional-client interactions leave the client only modestly satisfied with the output and highly unsatisfied with the process of getting there. It also contributes to a view of professionals as arrogant, inflexible, and lacking empathy.

Overcoming the
Responsibility Virus as a Professional

Of course not all professionals fall prey to the Responsibility Virus. Many have high-quality relationships with their clients in which the clients provide valuable insights in a collaborative process and come away delighted by both process and outcome.

But all can inoculate themselves from infection by integrating into their practice the four tools I have outlined:

1) Redefined Leadership

The professional will always be cast in a leadership role, but the professional's working definition of leadership is the critical distinction. At the outset, the professional must avoid signaling that leadership means taking over all responsibility.

On the contrary, the professional should signal that the skills and capabilities of the client are critically important to the task at hand, and that he or she intends to utilize these skills and capabilities to the fullest.

In the field of strategy consulting, almost all firms sell themselves on the basis of their *industry-specific* expertise. The consulting firm and clients both make the case that the consulting firm knows more of importance concerning the client's industry (say, airlines or pharmaceuticals) than the client does. This, despite the fact that the client lives in this industry every working day. By hiring on the basis of the consultant's industry expertise, the clients have implicitly signaled that they value the industry expertise of the consultant more than their own.

Mindful of these assumptions of superior knowledge, the consultant takes charge and does not look to the client for a meaningful contribution of insight. With no productive role to play, even though they work in the industry in question, clients are inclined to adopt the traditional definition of followership. They sit back to watch the consultant work, and the Virus is under way.

A much more productive stance for a strategy consultant is to sell expertise stemming from something more targeted and specific. They may be expert in transferring insights from other industries, or expert in a particular process. These complementary areas of expertise enable the consultant to be hired without an assumption that the consultant should take over and the client should passively await results. Instead, there can be a beneficial collaboration in which the client contributes industry and firm knowledge and the consultant provides the other-industry or process knowledge.

Drawing the client into a collaborative decisionmaking relationship almost always entails helping them over their initial uncertainty and fear. The consultant's position should not be "I'll take care of everything," but rather "I'll lead, but we're doing it together." If the client expresses fear and/or passivity in response, the professional must hang in and show both patience and resolve. The professional must be able to coax and cajole the client, however reluctant, into a genuinely collaborative relationship.

Collaborative behavior includes asking the client for help and support when the professional feels in trouble. This will almost certainly feel "unleaderly" to the professional, but it is a powerful and positive signal. The client invariably will step up to the plate to help out, and the act of helping out will encourage the client to overcome passivity and under-responsibility going forward.

If the client has difficulty accepting shared responsibility for choice-making, the professional can purposely act mildly helpless to encourage the client to step forward. Thanks to static conservation of responsibility, the natural reaction of the client to such a show of helplessness by the professional will be to surge forward and fill the gap. When the clients have done so once, they will be emboldened to try again. By using this technique the professional can nurse the client into taking on more responsibility and moving from the traditional to the redefined definition of followership.

2) The Choice Structuring Process

The professional must recognize the power of the Ladder of Inference to assist or undermine the professional relationship. In many respects, the professional is hired for his or her ladder of inference. The product they sell is choice-making that results from their analysis of data (whether medical, architectural, business, or otherwise), and the ability to draw meaningful inferences from that data. To the extent that this data selection and inference drawing is a private and mysterious process, the client will be unable to collaborate with the professional and will also see the result of the professional's thinking processes as mysterious and relatively inaccessible. They will be less likely to productively challenge a thinking process they don't even begin to understand.

So the take-charge doctor will be inclined to select the data salient to him, draw inferences from his experience, and tell the patient what he or she should do. The doctor will provide the minimum necessary data to the patient because the doctor's goal is to get the decision made as quickly and efficiently as possible. In this context, the patient will be at a loss to know how to protest if the course of action doesn't make complete sense. He or she can only guess at the true pattern of reasoning and will sense the doctor doesn't want a long, drawn-out conversation. For the patient, the bar for dissent is set very high, and many will go along and hold the doctor fully responsible for the decision if the outcome is less than ideal. In the case of my daughter's broken elbow, the doctor nodded wisely as I explained just how my daughter fell and what position her arm was in as she hit the ground. I had no way of knowing that he was ignoring everything I said and making a decision based on other data—the fact that 90 percent of elbow breaks happen a different way— and a hidden set of inferences based on that data.

Instead, collaborative professionals will make their thinking process clear, pointing out the data and the inferences that have led to their conclusions and their suggested actions. They will make their logic testable by the client and will work to draw out the other's data and inferences. If the professional's data and inferences do not compel the client, the professional will help the client design tests of those data and inferences. These tests will either help the client confirm and commit or enable the professionals to understand the error of their approach.

The collaborative professionals will understand that their product is not for them but for the client. That means that client understanding and commitment are critical. For this reason, the professional will attempt to do as little work as possible away from the client, because working together is the best way to build a mutual Ladder of Inference, which benefits from both the professional's expertise and the client's specific context.

3) The Responsibility Ladder

Whether they use the Responsibility Ladder explicitly or not, the professional should use its principles in interacting and collaborating with the client. The key is to recognize that the client's skills and capabilities are not static; rather, they are dynamic and can be either squelched or fostered constructively, depending on the attitude and actions of the professional.

There will always be substantial differences between the professional and client in their capabilities relative to the task at hand. If there is not a substantial difference, the wrong professional has been hired. But the size of the gap should not cause the professional to focus on the shortcomings of the client and, as a result, seize control.

If the professional can, instead, take a constructive developmental attitude, clients can both contribute to the resolution of the problem at hand and develop their own choice-making capabilities at the same time. The Responsibility Ladder can help set a target level of responsibility that stretches but does not break the client. The professional can do this with or without explicitly using the Ladder terminology.

If an architect tries to get a couple to come up with ideas for how to design the roofline so that it unifies their house, while also meeting building codes, they would probably fail miserably. But she can ask the couple to define in precise terms how they want to use the house they are building. That is likely to stretch their capabilities. If the architect asks them to identify the key design tradeoffs, she would be asking them a question they are incapable of answering. But if she talks them through the key design tradeoffs and asks for help in making those tradeoffs, she is likely to help them grow.

When clients are stretched, but not broken, it's remarkable how fast their capabilities can be developed. And the greater their choice-making capabilities, the better the outcome of the collaboration. In many respects, a key part of the professional's task is to build a better client in order to build a better service. To build a better client, the professional needs to bring the client up the Responsibility Ladder during the course of working with them.

4) The Frame Experiment

This is an important tool for the professional to have in his or her kit, because in professional relationships, frustration is a given, thanks to the potent combination of the capability gap, the client's fear, and the client's expectations. Depending on the clients and the particular situation, they will at some point become angry, petulant, helpless, opinionated, or otherwise uncooperative.

At the point of frustration, the professional is inclined to employ the classic frame—*Self: Correct; Client: Wrong; Task: Change the client's mind*—which, as we have seen, will only make the problem worse. The professional will sound more strident to the client, who will dig in or check out, causing the professional to become more strident still. The only likely result is a poor set of choices and an unhappy client.

The professional ideally should remain open to the possibility that the client is absolutely right and they themselves are absolutely wrong. If the professionals lose faith in the client, they have lost the ability to develop a productive relationship and will embark on a downward spiral. It is as simple as that. When they feel themselves becoming closed to the possibility that the client may be right, the professional can use the Frame Experiment to recover the situation. The revised frame need be no more complicated than—*Self: May be missing something; Client: May see something I don't; Task: Try to figure out whether they do.* The Frame Experiment allows the professional to reach out to the client and attempt to understand their data and their reasoning.

Empathy with the client's fear is also critical. Whether sick patient, embattled business executive, or worried house-builder, the client has every reason to be fearful and unclear as to what is going on. If the professionals assume that fear means incompetence, then they will dive more deeply into over-responsibility. If instead they recognize that client fear is a result of the client understanding that the task at hand is above his capability, and that he needs the professional's help in reaching up to a higher level, the professional will be less likely to react inappropriately.

The professionals also must remember that, no matter how hard they are working in their practice, the task is al-ways emotionally more difficult for the client. The profes-sionals must take into account how difficult it is for the client to put such an important issue in their hands. By em-ploying the frame experiment, the professional can listen to the clients long enough and hard enough to really under-stand their point of view, and then employ that perspective to better serve the clients by leading them to better choices.

CHAPTER 14

The Challenge for
Boards of Directors

"What were these fools up to?" Hans wondered. He was so angry he could barely speak. Four years ago he had been hired to turn around the fortunes of Grove Corporation, a once-proud firm whose position had eroded under successive generations of weak, self-satisfied management. He was the powerful chairman and CEO. But now the board of directors' newly formed strategy committee had just informed him—not suggested to him, but informed him—that the board was uncomfortable with his proposed strategy. Even worse, the directors wanted him to retain a consulting firm to review the strategy before voting on its ratification.

Hans had aggressively diversified Grove out of its slowly growing core business. Even within the core business he had repositioned the firm to improve its prospects. The board, which he had tried to upgrade to a more youthful and aggressive group, had done little to help him in the transformation. Once the directors had ousted his predecessor and hired Hans, they stepped completely into the background and had remained there ever since. They had ratified his initial strategy when he came to the job and had approved every acquisition he had proposed since.

Now, because the core business had softened more than expected, and several of the acquisitions weren't turning out the way he had planned, the board had suddenly turned on him. "My new strategy is clearly right," Hans fumed to himself. "And I had the courage to pursue it rather than run Grove into the ground. The board members have no idea what they're talking about. Despite that, they're taking actions that jeopardize the entire process I've been spearheading for four years!"

But Hans had no choice and, swallowing his pride, he hired the outside firm. The strategy was sound, he told the consultants, but the board simply didn't understand what had to be done. It wasn't easy. There had been and would continue to be bumps in the road, but his strategy was really the only sensible option. Despite Hans's forceful pitch, the consultants raised questions and suggested alternatives.

Hans saw this as an affront to his authority, which made him more obstreperous. He continued to make decisions without board review and aggressively proposed actions, including a huge write-off, that the board did not wish to consider before the conclusion of the consultants' review.

The board responded by giving the strategy committee increasing authority and arranged a weekend offsite at the conclusion of the consultants' work, during which the board as a whole, not just the CEO, would consider a range of strategic options and make a decision. Hans became increasingly strident in his criticism of the process and the board's new activist role. He insisted that it was his responsibility to review the work of the consultants and, based on his review, to come to the board with a strategy recommendation.

This aggressive stance alienated the board and undermined any remaining faith it had in his ability to complete the turnaround. Before the offsite, the board fired Hans and named one of its members chairman and interim CEO. The board took responsibility for the strategy decision. Based on the material presented and the debate at the offsite, the board made a number of critical strategic decisions, including—much to Hans's consternation—the very write-off Hans had been advocating.

The board also initiated a recruiting process for a new CEO and, after five months of searching, assisted by a leading global search firm, the board hired a new leader. The new man, Scott, was an experienced EVP from a much larger and more prestigious firm in a related industry. The board gave him an extremely favorable compensation package and a high level of authority for the management of the firm—authority that was eerily similar to that given to Hans upon his arrival in the executive suite. In anticipation of the new CEO's arrival, the strategy committee of the board disbanded and the strategy work stopped.

Scott went to work immediately on a new plan, with little input from or interaction with the board. Several months later he took the plan to the board for approval. It passed without alteration or even much discussion. The business papers covered the story of the new plan to turn around Grove with rapt enthusiasm. The board heaved a sigh of relief, seeing itself as having taken the steps necessary to ensure success for the shareholders of Grove. The directors had rid themselves of Hans, who never lived up to expectations, and replaced him with Scott, who was far more stable, tough-minded, and operational. With his new plan in place they could sit back, enjoy the positive press, and wait for the profit turnaround to take shape.

Sadly for the board, Scott, and the shareholders of Grove Corp., nothing of the sort occurred. Under Scott's leadership, profits continued to trend downward and the stock with it. Within eighteen months, the stock had dropped to less than half of its level at the time of Scott's arrival. Analysts were no longer complaining about the "rich package of stock options" that the board had awarded Scott, since none of those options would be worth a penny for the foreseeable future. However, shareholders were furious and began to call for the new man's head. The directors began to wonder if they had been fooled again. Scott seemed increasingly like another Hans. How could that be?

Boards of directors are highly prone to the Responsibility Virus with respect to senior management, but particularly with respect to their CEOs.

Most CEOs find working with their board to be an activity that does not contribute to shareholder or customer satisfaction. They feel that the board is just another constituency to be managed so that it doesn't constrain their ability to function. In twenty years of working with CEOs, I have not found one who would have objected strenuously to their board being abolished. The problems stemmed not from any awkward personal interaction or lack of admiration, but from the nature of the relationship.

As a result, many boards are unable to fulfill their governance role on behalf of shareholders. Shareholders are often left shaking their heads after a precipitous corporate down-turn, wondering, "*Where were the directors?*" They were there, but not in a productive relationship with management.

Shareholders' and managers' interests are not inherently aligned. It is the function of corporate governance to align these interests, so that managers' actions are undertaken in the best interests of the shareholders, whom the boards of directors represent.[1]

The challenge of monitoring top management performance is not inconsequential, even for talented, experienced board members. Board members need to possess deep knowledge about the organization itself, and about the industry in which the organization operates, as well as knowledge about corporate governance.

Moreover, given that the CEO is often a prominent board member—chairman in some situations, chairman of the compensation committee in other situations—struggles between the chairman/CEO and the rest of the board are quite common—giving rise to the Responsibility Virus.[2]

Hans's relationship with the Grove board started out in typical fashion. The board brought him in from the outside to replace the previous failed CEO. Grove had been such a stable performer that it was a proverbial "widows and orphans" stock held by many individual shareholders. It had long operated on virtual autopilot and the board functioned in a hands-off fashion. When performance started to sour under the previous CEO, the board came under criticism for the first time in anyone's memory. Embarrassed, the board took charge aggressively and, in a high-profile move, went outside to hire the new CEO, whom they announced with great fanfare. In the wake of their previous embarrassment and pain, the directors were delighted to repose a high level of faith and responsibility in Hans.

In the language of the Responsibility Ladder, the board gave wide-ranging Level 1 authority to Hans. He was able to make most decisions on his own or with the help of his management team, and only inform the board afterwards. Only on a narrow range of issues—for example, a sizable acquisition—was Hans mandated by longstanding governance procedures to come with a recommendation for board approval—that is, Level 2 responsibility. However, in these situations, the board's standard procedure was to approve the request without much, if any, scrutiny. Every single acquisition Hans had proposed since his arrival had been ratified.

Hans's relationship with the board had evolved to the point that he would never consider going to them, or even to individual directors, on a Level 3 basis—that is, options but no recommendation—or, heaven forbid, anything below that level.

Boards typically collude implicitly with the CEO to reinforce such behavior by accepting, if not encouraging, Level 1 behavior and by readily ratifying Level 2 recommendations. Indeed, a very common criticism of boards is that they are passive ratifiers of top management decisions, because of the obvious interpersonal and sometimes pecuniary costs of openly confronting top managers and criticizing their decisions.[3]

Take a situation in which a director feels queasy about a CEO's decision brought to the board for confirmation. Unless the director in question is the retired CEO (which sometimes happens, although most CEOs try not to allow former CEOs on their board), the CEO knows much more about the business than the queasy director. The queasy director fears, therefore, that he or she is more likely to *lose, not win* the subsequent argument. And the director knows there will be an argument because the CEO is used to having everything ratified and won't like the queasy director's questioning. As that argument ensues, the situation may *get out of control*, which could make it impossible to *stay rational*. And, of course, all of the above would be *highly embarrassing* for all involved, but especially for the director who has spoken up.

Trying to ameliorate such situations with financial incentive, giving stock and stock options to make board members feel more like "owners," ignores the immediate, interpersonal costs. Research underscores the human tendency to discount costs that are far away in the future much more sharply than we discount costs that are imminent.[4] Thus a loss in stock value—something that may be felt next quarter or next year—can pale in comparison with the immediate cost of cutting down an aggressive CEO, and, even worse, undergoing the public embarrassment of losing the argument.

So directors tend to keep their concerns to themselves and act as passive followers despite their formal authority and their personal seniority. This is highly baffling to outsiders, who tend to ask, especially after precipitous crashes, *"With all those powerful directors and all the governance procedures in place, why didn't the board do something? Anything? They fiddled while Rome burned!"*

The answer is the Responsibility Virus. As the directors back off, the CEO watches this passive behavior and assumes that he or she has no real choice but to seize even more responsibility. The CEO increasingly treats the board as an afterthought, generally assuming that all his recommendations will be promptly rubber-stamped. This stance is quite handy for the CEO as well. He or she manages to *win, not lose, maintain control, avoid embarrassment,* and *stay rational* while the board accomplishes the same goals.

However, as this pattern of behavior rolls forward, problematic side effects emerge. First, as board acquiescence becomes ever more ensconced, raising any question at all becomes an increasingly daunting task. The longer the tradition of silence persists, the more awkward it feels to break it. So directors suppress their worrisome issues.

The CEO watches this behavior and becomes more certain that the board can't add any value to his thinking. As a consequence, the CEO accords the board less and less weight. The board watches this behavior and wonders why its CEO is becoming so imperious.

The misunderstanding and mistrust grow simultaneously with the growth in the gap between responsibilities. As the board takes on duties farther and farther below the directors' capabilities, the waste of talent can be breathtaking. Imagine a dozen or more CEOs, chairmen, senior lawyers and bankers, as well as former political leaders, sitting around a table and rubber-stamping decisions. It is almost as if the directors and the CEO wait for a failure to emerge to get them out of this tragic pattern.

And so it was at Grove. Fresh from the feeling of losing, ceding control to angry shareholders, and feeling profoundly embarrassed by the failure of the previous CEO, the board seized control, sacked him, and hired Hans. In doing so, the board flipped from under-responsibility to over-responsibility. But then just as quickly, it flipped back to under-responsibility by handing over everything to Hans. From that moment onward, Hans found it easiest to seize more responsibility and allow the board to take on less. Directors became ever more uncomfortable, yet remained silent. Hans became ever more aggressive, while wondering about the quality of the directors.

And although both Hans and the board designed their actions so as to avoid *losing, ceding control, being embarrassed,* and *becoming emotional*, these are the very things that happened to both parties within a span of four years. The board was seen as having shown poor governance. It was under huge pressure by dissident shareholders to change the board composition. And it was embarrassed in the press and at shareholders' meetings. Hans was painted as a failed CEO. His total control of the leadership of Grove was under attack, and he was living with the embarrassment of being skewered in the business press. As usual, those afflicted with the Responsibility Virus produced the exact opposite of their intended goals.

When failure strikes, the board tends to move abruptly from passivity to micro-management. In this new mode, it bans Level 1 behavior by the CEO and often discourages Level 2 responsibility as well. It does so by questioning the CEO's recommendations. Typically, the board explicitly or implicitly asks the CEO to drop down to Level 3 (coming to the board with options, not recommendations) or Level 4 responsibility (coming to the board for help in structuring the problem at hand) on most issues.

Directors are likely to hold the CEO largely responsible for past failure and absolve themselves of most of the blame. They tend to be quite self-satisfied and unreflective as they point to the CEO's imperious behavior and blame him or her for not seeking the counsel of the board and for ramming through recommendations without checking whether board members had real concerns. With few exceptions, the directors simply do not see how their behaviors encouraged, reinforced, and exacerbated the behavior they now criticize. This obliviousness helps this phenomenon occur in board after board.

When the board takes control, the CEO can quickly become confused and demoralized in this new situation. CEOs typically have no experience in playing the Level 3/Level 4 role on which the board now insists. They have little respect for the directors, who have been so passive. And the lack of respect is genuine, not just anger-based. They may have watched the board members rubber-stamp the very decisions they now criticize, and add no perceptible value. They may genuinely see the directors as incapable of helping and doubt whether shareholder interests are being served by the directors' newfound enthusiasm.

The CEO quickly chafes under the board's newly imposed authority. In this scenario, CEOs see themselves as being forced to check every decision at a time when, due to the failure or pressure, decisionmaking speed and quality are of critical importance. And they have to check with directors they see as lacking competence to help. Eventually they become so demoralized they resign, or the board becomes so upset that it fires the CEO.

Hans saw his board as a bunch of meddling know-nothings and made that view patently clear to anyone who would listen. He saw radical action, including a big write-off, as essential to survival, and quick execution as a no-brainer. When the board decided to postpone the write-off against his wishes, he questioned its dedication to saving Grove. He felt that the consultants' study was unnecessary—he knew what he needed to know—and waiting for its results before acting was reckless and foolish.

In short order, the relationship with the board became so strained that the board saw a fundamental impasse and thought it time for a new leader. In coming to that conclusion, they focused almost exclusively on Hans's culpability. Hans was arrogant. Hans didn't listen to the board. Hans was inflexible. Hans didn't know how to manage the Board. In this crisis, Hans was being reckless. At no point did they look carefully at their own responsibility in creating the board norms that made it easiest for Hans to follow the path he followed. This failure to reflect would sow the seeds of the next crisis.

Rationalizing that the previous leader "just wasn't up to the task," boards search for a new CEO, typically at a higher compensation level, because "that is what it will take to attract the kind of talent we need." In order to attract their new savior, the board tends to hand the incoming CEO as much if not more authority than was exercised by the CEO they have just deposed, retreating back into the comfortable world of passive followership. In doing so, the board invites the Responsibility Virus back into the board-CEO relationship and sets itself up for another round of failure.

At Grove, the board engaged in a global search with one of the world's leading recruitment firms. It hired a new CEO at a compensation level that would have made the old CEO faint. Immediately upon bringing in the new blood, the strategy committee disbanded and turned over all responsibility to the new CEO. That was OK, they told themselves, because this guy was really talented. Not like the flawed and imperious Hans!

It was as if the episode four years earlier had never occurred. Untreated, the Virus creates never-ending cycles of handing over and then reclaiming untrammeled authority, with endless cycles of failure and recrimination in between.

Tools for Overcoming the Challenge to Board Effectiveness

Boards of directors need to use the four tools to combat the Responsibility Virus if they are to succeed in providing the governance for which they were created in the first place.

1) The Responsibility Ladder

This is the key tool for the board to use in guiding its thinking and forming its relationship with its CEO, and the critical element is flexibility. The board must internalize the reality that no single level of responsibility is right for all choices. When all choices are treated equally, the CEO and board are likely to drift to a Level 1 habit for the CEO. As soon as that habit sets in, embarrassment is threatened if the board wants to take greater responsibility and the CEO lesser responsibility on a given choice or set of choices. The threat of embarrassment tends to cause the board to back off and accept Level 1 behavior, even when directors think that they should intervene. Only when a crisis makes engaging with the CEO the lesser of two embarrassing evils do directors step up to higher, and appropriate, responsibility. And as was the case at Grove, that moment is often far too late for the downward spiral to be averted. Hence boards need to figure out how to be proactive in a way that doesn't trigger the Responsibility Virus.

To accomplish this goal, the board needs to learn to walk up and down the Responsibility Ladder in a way that does not give rise to embarrassment. It needs to practice, establishing issues on which it explicitly asks the CEO to take Level 3 or Level 4 responsibility. For example, the chairman can ask the CEO to come forward with options (Level 3) for the board to consider on a certain issue. This sets up the proper expectation for the board and the CEO so the CEO doesn't feel weak when he or she comes forward with something less definitive than usual. It is important for the board to ask the CEO to operate at lower levels of the Ladder in good times, not just times of crisis, because if it is the latter the CEO will think (probably rightly) that the board request is a reflection of its lack of confidence in him or her.

In parallel, the CEO needs to be able to ask for board help—that is, come to the board at Level 3 or Level 4—without fear of embarrassment, without feeling as if he or she is losing. The CEO needs to feel encouraged to drop down to a lower level when facing challenging issues and to consider this a sign of strength of thinking rather than a sign of weakness. Ironically, at Grove, Hans never came to the board with anything but Level 1, but that resulted in his being seen as weak—that is, oblivious—rather than strong.

Neither board nor CEO should feel they are losing control by moving away from Level 1 choice-making by the CEO. To get to this point, the board and the CEO must have a mutual understanding of the Responsibility Ladder and a commitment to use it in their interactions. Both the CEO and directors should feel empowered to operate at any level on the Ladder and should practice at various levels depending on the issue at hand.

Practice at various levels will help both the board and CEO fine-tune their responsibilities to their capabilities. Avoiding periods of over-responsibility and under-responsibility will grow their choice-making capabilities. The directors will become more capable board members and the CEO will become a better CEO.

The adoption of the Responsibility Ladder in a firm's board-CEO relationship is no small task. It is best accomplished through a developmentally oriented chairman who is keen to check not only the products and procedures of board interactions, but also the decision processes that take place at the board level.[5] It is difficult for this to occur when the chairman is also the CEO, so this provides yet another good reason to split these two important roles.

2) Redefinition of Leadership/Followership

The board-CEO relationship is in many ways a strange one with respect to leadership-followership. Either side could be seen as taking the lead or bringing up the rear. The board could be seen as leading because it has the authority to hire, fire, and compensate the CEO. However, the CEO could be seen as leading because he or she holds the bulk of the real decisionmaking authority. In many cases, the CEO is also a prominent member of the audit, investment, and compensation committees, the very committees in which the bulk of the board's decision rights are vested.

In many respects, this relationship is perfectly suited to the redefinition described earlier. As we saw, the stance and goal of redefined leaders and followers are identical. Redefined leaders and followers both seek to:

- Split responsibility through dialogue,
- Apportion responsibility in keeping with capabilities,
- Make apportionment discussable, and
- Subject performance to testing by both parties.

At the board level, redefined leadership and followership would represent true partnership between the board and the CEO, in that there would be no clear leader and no clear follower. This entails shared but different responsibility and differing *levels* of responsibility, depending on the choice at hand and the relative capabilities.

This redefinition depends on a more open dialogue between board and CEO than is characteristic, particularly with respect to the sharing of responsibility. With such a re-definition of leadership and followership, neither side can or will feel comfortable seizing or abdicating responsibility. They will, instead, be comfortable with varying levels of responsibility that are more fine-tuned, and the shareholders will be the beneficiaries of this state.

3) The Frame Experiment

Even with the best of intentions boards and CEOs will come to a point of disagreeing with one another and beginning to miscommunicate, even mistrust one another. That's when the board needs to be able to reframe the CEO in order to hold a productive conversation.

The unproductive frame might be—

CEO: Insubordinate, independent, disrespectful;
Board: Ignored, disrespected, insulted;
Task: Bring the CEO into line.

Or in the opposite situation, it might be—

CEO: Weak, dependent, unleaderly;
Board: Forced to make all the decisions;
Task: Get the CEO to take responsibility.

In either case, the board frame needs to change to something of the following sort—

CEO: Acting in ways we don't understand and which undermine our confidence;
Board: May have a valid concern, but may not see important things that the CEO sees;

Task: Engage the CEO in a dialogue that helps both
sides understand the situation and take action if
necessary.

Access to the Frame Experiment tool will help the board to
use the Responsibility Ladder on an ongoing basis, rather than
becoming fearful about the CEO and his/her actions to such an
extent that the board feels compelled to take unilateral action
instead of action that stems from a productive dialogue. Of
course, given natural proclivities to look for confirming evidence for a frame, which may be operational for both the CEO
and board members, it will take two to tango in the frame experiment. If the CEO does not take the frame experiment seriously, then his or her behaviors may very quickly come to be
interpreted by the board as evidence for the fact that the CEO
has reverted back to the old, uncollaborative frame.

4) The Choice Structuring Process

Boards and CEOs have to make complex and difficult decisions at high levels. These choices often embody complicated
streams of logic that can be easily misunderstood, which in
turn can result in the development of counterproductive
frames and the potential downward spiral they produce.

Adding to the confusion, a CEO has ample opportunity
and incentive to veil his or her logic in a maze of technical
jargon. Knowing this fact, board members often have every
reason to be suspicious of the CEO's policy recommendations—both of their form and their content.

Boards can use the Choice Structuring Process to ask
what they would have to believe for them to be confident in,
for example, the CEO's proposal coming forward. If they
make these conditions specific, then the CEO can understand
the standard of proof required by the board.

This establishes the same kind of process used in science to distinguish between valid and flawed theories. Boards can reasonably insist that the strategy choices of the CEO be subjected to empirical testing. Thus, boards can be expected to produce logical audits of the process by which top managers—and especially the CEO—make decisions.[6]

This process is superior to the situation in which the board leaves its reasoning vague or even, in the worst cases, simply says no or yes without revealing its logic. With thorough understanding of each other's logic, the board and CEO are more inclined to work collaboratively on gaining sufficient confidence to either ratify or dismiss an initiative or proposal. In addition, neither side is inclined to see the other as being unilateral and controlling. Instead each side will grow to better understand the thinking process of the other side. This will produce the additional benefit of both sides being better equipped to utilize the Responsibility Ladder to apportion responsibilities, because to apportion responsibilities both sides must understand the capabilities of the other side.

By utilizing the four tools in combination, especially the Responsibility Ladder and the Redefinition of Leadership/Followership, boards and CEOs can create a fluid environment for choice-making in which the best capabilities are brought to bear and the spirit of partnership is reinforced. With these four tools in use, there is a lower probability of flawed decisions being ratified and causing the organization harm. In addition to making better decisions by employing the best current capabilities, an environment featuring these tools will develop the choice-making skills of both boards and CEOs. Overall, the use of the tools has the potential to transform boards of directors from being a hassle to be endured, into a tool for better management.

CHAPTER 15

Fighting the
Virus in Everyday Life

Thus far we have talked about the Responsibility Virus in the context of senior executives in large organizations. But the Virus is equally prevalent between husbands and wives, teachers and students, parents and children, friends and co-workers.

The same problems usually ensue—undermining of collaboration, build-up of misunderstanding and mistrust, and atrophy of skills. And in many respects the costs are even higher. When the Responsibility Virus causes misunderstanding and mistrust between a husband and wife or parent and child, that's not just a loss of profit or market share but a deep wound at a very personal level. That's why fighting the Responsibility Virus in daily life is as important as fighting it on the job.

Fortunately the same tools can be applied to the Responsibility Virus in everyday life as in organizational life. The

Choice Structuring Process, the Frame Experiment, the Responsibility Ladder, and the Redefinition of Leadership and Followership need to be applied in a somewhat less formal manner, but they can be applied nonetheless, either singularly or in combination, depending on the situation in question.

Leading with the Responsibility Ladder

Robert and Farah are college sweethearts, living together in an apartment in Cambridge while Robert attends Harvard Business School and Farah gets her degree at the Kennedy School of Government. It is first year for both and they are being worked hard in their respective core programs. In particular, Robert, who holds down a part-time job, feels pressured by time. After class ends at 3:30 p.m. he goes to work and gets back at about 7:00 p.m. pretty tired. Nonetheless, Monday through Thursday he has cases that need to be prepared for class next day.

Farah feels pressure of a different sort. Never a fan of math, she stayed away from quantitative courses as an undergraduate. She chose to attend the Kennedy School to pursue her interest in international development, and while her program is not quantitative overall, it required a quantitative methods course in the first year. There was no way to avoid it, and a B- was the lowest grade allowed for students hoping to pass into second year. The problem was that, unlike most of the other courses in which class participation counted considerably, and extra effort on papers could leverage one's grade, in this course the answers were simply right or wrong. This was the course that tended to weed students out of the program. So Farah was unnerved by the fact that she might actually fail.

Almost every day Robert would come home to find Farah with head in hands, elbows on the kitchen table, struggling with her QuantMethods assignments. Robert would pull out the three cases for next day and start the three to five hours of preparation his own courses demanded. But he was far too much in love to watch Farah struggle alone, especially when she pounded the table and ran crying into the bedroom. Robert was a math whiz and he knew he could help. He went to the bedroom, got Farah to come back to her work, and started talking her through the first problem, a probabilities question. Farah followed along and could see why Robert's approach made lots of sense. Robert rushed a bit through the rest of the problems because by now it was 9:30 and he had barely started his first case. However, true love meant staying up late to help your sweetheart, didn't it?

As the days passed, the routine became more and more established. Rather than struggle through the math on her own, Farah would get the rest of her work out of the way before Robert came home. When he came in the door, she would have her QuantMethods assignment spread out on the table, signaling to him that she was ready to start.

Though mightily in love, Robert started to resent the assumption that part of his job in life was to help Farah with her work every night, no matter how tired or busy he was. His workload was huge, and none of his classmates had both a job and the need to do someone else's work in addition to their own. He started rushing through Farah's work more quickly, glossing over her questions and blowing past her quizzical looks. Farah sensed his annoyance but didn't really understand it. Knowing he had lots of work to do, she decided to let him go as fast as he wanted even if it meant not asking questions and getting lost occasionally as she tried to follow his thinking.

Robert found her behavior disconcerting as well. "Doesn't she care at all about learning the material?" he wondered. "I hate being the surrogate for Farah in this course. It must be in the program for a reason. She's not going to learn anything if she just sits there and watches me do the problem sets. And lord knows I could use the time to prepare my cases. I get by, but guys like Tony, Eric, and Sanjay are easily twice as prepared as I am. No wonder they shine in class. I wonder if Farah is really committed to the program or just wants the degree to pad her resume."

Farah's problem-set assignments always came back with passing grades, but on her first mid-term in Quant-Methods she received a C, a failing grade, and it counted for more than all of the assignments combined. It also foreshadowed the final. Robert realized that his worst fears were coming true. He was more engaged in the course than Farah, but he couldn't take the exams for her. This was heading in a bad direction, and it wasn't doing anything for their relationship either!

Robert and Farah were experiencing the Responsibility Virus, domestic version. At Farah's first flinch—tears in the bedroom—Robert leaped into action and helped with the problem set. Rather than respond cautiously and minimally, he leapt in with both feet and took charge. As he increasingly assumed the leading role, she increasingly backed off, until he felt he was doing the course himself, and she felt lost. Along the way, Robert began questioning Farah's motives and commitment to learning, and Farah began to see a sharp and sarcastic side of Robert that she hadn't seen before and didn't much like. Rather than pulling them closer together, the work on QuantMethods pushed them farther apart.

What could they do in the wake of the C grade on the midterm? They could lead with the Responsibility Ladder tool.

Robert could lead by saying:

Farah, I realize I've contributed to this C. I've been focusing too much on getting the problem sets done and not enough on your learning, which is of course the point. Going forward, I'd like to try to do the absolute minimum possible to help you when you're stuck and leave the rest to you. You'll learn faster that way. Sometimes I see you struggling with the problem itself, and I realize you don't know how to think about it. Is it a probabilities problem or a distribution problem or an optimization problem? Other times you understand the problem, but you have trouble figuring out how to apply the quantitative method to it. In other cases, you understand the problem, and the quantitative method, but you have trouble with a calculation. The farther along you take it without me, the better for your learning.

Let's make a ladder and you identify where you are on a problem when you get stuck. Let's say the lowest rung will entail understanding the problem. On the second rung will be knowing the quantitative method to apply. On the third rung, performing the calculation, and on the fourth rung checking the calculation. Maybe there are more rungs. I'll help you only on the rung where you're stuck and leave the rest to you. We'll keep track of how high up that ladder you get on your own. If you're moving up the ladder before you get stuck, we'll know you're learning and can have confidence you'll do well on the exam. If you keep getting stuck at the lower rungs, we'll know you need something more.

This move by Robert could create a language system for discussing in a more sophisticated and granular way the kind of help Farah needs. (Farah could initiate the same suggestion, though in her under-responsible mode she might be less capable of constructing the suggestion, much less having the courage to make it.) If they adopt the modified Responsibility Ladder approach, they will find themselves working together in a more collaborative fashion and both will understand much better what Farah needs to move forward.

Leading with the Responsibility Ladder makes sense in this situation because the crux of the problem is the inappropriate distribution of responsibilities. Difficulty collaborating on a decision or the definition of leadership might also be present, but to a lesser degree.

However, depending on how deeply ingrained the sense of misunderstanding and even mistrust has become, it may be necessary to lead with a Frame Experiment. If Robert is so convinced that Farah doesn't care about learning and just wants him to do her work for her, then he will be unable to craft the suggested course of action above. Instead, he would have to lead with a positive reframing of Farah before diving into the Responsibility Ladder. (Again the same holds for Farah if she is to initiate. She may have to reframe Robert as other than impatient, sarcastic, and overbearing in order to make the Responsibility Ladder suggestion.)

Leading with the
Choice Structuring Process

Tim and Wendy are a pair of lawyers, married with children aged eight and eleven. Tim is a litigator at a large firm, while Wendy is a corporate securities lawyer for a regulatory agency. They have grown out of their current house and Wendy in particular wants to buy something bigger. Tim agrees, but in fact he's largely indifferent. He doesn't see the faults of the existing house to be as big a deal as Wendy does.

Wendy lines up a prospective real estate agent, but Tim, who's working on a big, intense case, can't be at the first meeting. He gives Wendy his proxy, but she worries that Tim should be there. Not wanting to slow down the process, however, she sets aside her qualms and makes the appointment.

At the meeting, the two women discuss price range, location, and type of house, and then the agent goes to work and arranges visits to ten houses. Wendy takes a vacation day to tour them all, but Tim can only arrange to grab a couple hours between meetings. With his limited time, he sees only two houses, and he turns up his nose at both. Wendy agrees on one—she thought it was hideous—but she rather liked the other. However, she does not put it on the list of four "call back" houses she thinks warrant second visits together with Tim.

Scheduling the visits is tough with Tim's case going full-tilt, and by the time they get them scheduled, one house has sold, one that Wendy really liked. By now she's getting upset. "It's not as if I have no commitments and lots of time on my hands," she thinks. "I had to use a vacation day and I've been on the phone for hours, and now one of the two best houses has been sold out from underneath us. Tim is not lifting a finger to help."

They visit the three remaining houses and Tim doesn't find any one of them worth bidding on. In the first case, the street is too busy. The second is too far from the subway, and the third "doesn't feel right."

By the end of the appointment at the third house, Wendy is livid, and the real estate agent is rolling her eyeballs—not one of these criteria Tim just invoked was mentioned in the initial meeting. Wendy argues for her favorite house, but Tim just looks pained and makes it clear that he can't make himself go along with her on it.

Tim has to race back to the office, leaving Wendy and the agent to talk. "We aren't getting anywhere," Wendy sighs. "I'm not prepared to waste more time working like this. I don't have the energy to search for perfectly fine houses only to have Tim nix them for reasons I don't even understand. I really don't think he wants to move, so he's going to find a reason to nix every house."

"I hate to say this," the agent responds. "But I don't have time to waste either. I think you two need to decide whether you're buying or not."

Wendy thinks about it for a minute and says: "Don't worry. I'm just going to tell Tim that he's too busy and that he needs to give me his proxy. I'll take into account all his concerns and criteria, but I'm going to make the call."

"OK, I can live with that," the agent says. But secretly, she wonders what sort of fur will fly when they get down to a decision.

The Responsibility Virus can extinguish collaboration within couples as easily as between colleagues. When Wendy sees Tim flinch early on, she grabs more responsibility, at the same time resenting Tim for not contributing to this important decision. But then the more responsibility she takes, the more Tim recedes.

The problem is that Wendy is left to guess at what Tim most wants in a house, and, like most of us, she is an imperfect guesser. Tim doesn't like the houses she picked or is annoyed at the degree to which he feels swept along, but he rejects all the choices without providing clarity about his reasoning.

Stressful and expensive life decisions call for collaboration in the worst way, but the Responsibility Virus undermines it. To make a good choice, Wendy and Tim need to work together to build a shared definition of what they want in a house. One or the other alone is not capable of fully developing the optimal definition. Tim retreats more and more, taking with him the personal insights only he can provide. Wendy increasingly fills the vacuum by taking charge. As they migrate to opposite extremes, the Virus adds to the misunderstanding and tension. In the end Wendy ups the ante even further, reducing Tim's potential contribution to near zero.

But rather than push Tim out entirely, Wendy could use a variant of the Choice Structuring Process to engage him in the thinking process.

She could lead with something like the following:

Tim, I don't think we understand the choices we need to make on a house well enough to move ahead. Based on the houses we've both seen to date, let's try to identify the key options we have, because we know we won't be able to get *everything we want without paying far more than we can afford. For example, we may need to accept a slightly busier street in order to get the size and quality we need. If we laid out the four or five options, we could think them through and ask, what would have to be true for one of the options to outrank all the rest? I mean, we might be willing to accept a busier-than-optimal street if we can get a three-bedroom detached with a garage and under $25,000 in renovations required before moving in. Or maybe none of those things would compensate for a busy street and we could set an absolute level on how busy the street can be.*

I think if we spent a little time identifying the options and "reverse-engineering" how we feel about them together, I would have a much better chance of testing the houses that I see against these joint criteria. That way you would likely be much less disappointed when I show you houses that I think are candidates, and I won't get depressed because you reject everything I come up with. And then, each time we reject a house, we'll learn something together about how to refine our choice process.

This move by Wendy could create a way to engage in a collaborative dialogue that helps each of them understand their reasoning. They may well learn things about each other's preferences that would have taken many house visits to recognize or would have never come out. Such hidden logic could have resulted in Tim's rejecting houses for reasons that Wendy never understood—and vice versa—creating fertile ground for guessing about some nefarious reason (for example, Tim doesn't really want to move).

In addition to increasing understanding and furthering collaboration, this approach would have the effect of dragging Tim to a higher level of responsibility. Although in this case it may be appropriate for Wendy to take the lead responsibility, employing the Choice Structuring Tool could prevent her from migrating to an extreme.

However, Wendy won't be able to make much use of the Choice Structuring Process or the Responsibility Ladder if she harbors suspicions that Tim doesn't want to buy a house at all. Depending on how deep down the sense of misunderstanding has gone, she may need to lead with a Frame Experiment.

Leading with the Frame Experiment

Eliza and Tory are longtime cycling buddies. Ever since they roomed together at college, they've done a long bike trek together every second Saturday, rain or shine, with the Bay Area terrain offering them a perfect and varied environment.

Eliza had always been the more organized and opinionated of the two and Tory the more happy-go-lucky. As a result, Eliza usually suggested the route for the day, including timing and a place for lunch. Typically Tory's response was "Great, sounds good to me." When Eliza tried to engage Tory in discussion about the choices they might consider within the overall route she was suggesting, Tory would be inclined to respond, "Whatever you think."

In due course, Eliza stopped asking Tory for her opinions and just e-mailed her the meeting time and location and expected Tory to show up, which she did. The routes were sometimes a bit tough for Tory, who was not as strong a cyclist as Eliza, but in general she didn't complain.

One Saturday, Tory arrived at the appointed time and location to find not just Eliza but also Eliza's friend Helen.

Helen was an even stronger cyclist than Eliza and that worried Tory, who knew this was going to be a taxing ride. She also worried about losing the camaraderie with Eliza, riding side by side and catching up on the previous two weeks.

It turned out that the course wasn't too tough, but it wasn't as much fun with a threesome. It took up too much road space to ride three wide so someone was always the odd woman out. However, as the months went by, more of Eliza's friends showed up, and some of the rides seemed much more tuned to these newcomers than to Tory. And Eliza never even asked! She just took Tory for granted. She was getting really bossy, it seemed. Just an e-mail with orders, no discussion and no way to know who would be on the ride and whether Tory enjoyed their company or not. They used to be so close, and now Eliza was turning into an imperious, bossy woman who had taken their joint tradition and made it hers for the experimenting.

Tory began to make excuses for missing the rides. Eliza was surprised, and she missed having Tory along. When she encouraged her friend to ignore the excuse du jour and come along, Tory felt as if she was being pushed around, which got her back up more. Eliza was not accustomed to sharp responses from Tory and wondered why she was defending such feeble excuses so aggressively.

The Responsibility Virus strikes again. Tory has descended into a fully under-responsible state and Eliza has filled the vacuum by being over-responsible. Every time Tory agreed with a route plan without making a comment, Eliza interpreted it as a signal that Tory didn't care. In fact Tory did care, just not as much as Eliza did, and Tory actually liked Eliza's taste in routes well enough that there was never anything to discuss. Based on the signal inadvertently sent and received, Eliza acted more and more unilaterally. In due course, she accidentally violated something about which Tory had a strong opinion—the intimacy of the twosome on their long rides. But by this time Eliza was doing all the planning without bothering to ask, because she had long assumed that Tory didn't have an opinion.

Tory began to develop a frame as follows:

Self: Unappreciated and overlooked old friend
Eliza: Domineering, uncaring, and previously close friend
Task: Distance myself from the hurt of this relationship gone awry

Eliza in turn developed the following:

Self: Dutiful and under-appreciated cycling organizer
Tory: Increasingly hard-to-understand person who seems to be hiding something
Task: Disengage from this frustrating person

Given the mutual hurt and misunderstanding, it could be helpful for one or both to engage in a Frame Experiment. Tory could seek to meet with Eliza with the following Frame Experiment in mind:

Self: Hiding my true feelings and perhaps contributing to a misunderstanding
Eliza: Trying to plan and organize as she always has and perhaps completely unaware of my increasing disenchantment with the cycling
Task: Try to understand Eliza's thinking better and share mine with her in hopes of restoring the closeness of the relationship

A Frame Experiment led by Tory could help her approach Eliza in a fashion that causes Eliza to respond constructively and start unraveling the growing web of untested attributions. It would be likely to create a dialogue between the two old friends that would result in Tory's taking on a healthier level of responsibility in planning and organizing the outings. Also, it would help Eliza understand what aspects of the relationship are most important to Tory. Finally, it may have the positive result of helping Eliza understand how her over-responsibility can get her into trouble as well.

In this case, given the emotional disengagement already under way, it probably is necessary to lead with the Frame Experiment. Attempting to dive in with the Choice Structuring Process or the Responsibility Ladder would probably not work because the emotional issues first need to be cooled down.

Leading with the Redefinition of Leadership and Followership

Larry and Trudy have been married for twelve years. Trudy is a gifted interior designer with a renowned sense of color and space. She works on her own because she has never liked the constraints of a bigger firm. Larry works in an engineering consulting company where he's recently been offered partnership.

While Larry's larger shop has a support staff, Trudy's business is not so simple to manage. There are contracts to finalize, workers to pay, bills to collect, proposals to write, and so on. Larry would watch the paperwork pile up on Trudy's desk in her home office and start to worry.

Inevitably the bank or the IRS or a client would send a chilling letter and there would be a crisis. At this point Larry leaps into action and single-handedly wrestles the problem to the ground, often by working through the backlog of unpaid bills, tax notices, and contracts on Trudy's desk. The work takes long hours, frequently cutting into sleep and ruining weekends.

Sometimes the solutions require tough negotiations with suppliers or clients and, when Trudy hears back with complaints from one of the parties, she asks Larry why he needs to be so aggressive. At this point Larry almost loses his temper. "If you actually paid any attention to this stuff on an ongoing basis, I wouldn't have to fix everything and we wouldn't have anybody upset. But all you want to do is the interior designing."

However, when the crisis of the moment blows over, Trudy goes back to business as usual and Larry goes back to his work, knowing in the back of his mind that he will be jumping on the hand grenade again sometime soon, feeling powerless to avoid another crisis.

In this case study of the Responsibility Virus it is likely that:

1. Crises will perpetuate;
2. Trudy will not build the skills necessary to avoid crises;
3. Larry will grow increasingly resentful of the need to keep bailing Trudy out of crises, even as she criticizes the way he does it; and
4. Trudy will grow increasingly resentful of Larry's attitude toward her.

In due course, either Larry will get so annoyed with the bailout requirement that he will refuse to help and there will be a cataclysm, or his work on tackling crises will cause him to fail elsewhere in his life.

It may be helpful for both parties to redefine the roles in their specific predicament. Little can be done until Larry redefines valuable leadership. Larry's current definition has all of the classically counterproductive features:

- He splits responsibility in an entirely unilateral manner as soon as evidence of a crisis presents itself;
- He seizes all of the responsibility for overcoming the crisis;
- He does it without any discussion of what he has decided to do; and
- He subjects his performance only to private testing and bristles at Trudy's criticizing him in any way.

These are all classically "manly" leadership features, but they don't actually provide meaningful long-term help, especially to Trudy.

To get out of their downward spiral, Larry will need to embrace a different definition of leadership with respect to Trudy:

- He splits responsibility by way of a discussion with Trudy over who should do what in order to overcome the crisis;
- He splits the responsibility with Trudy so as to cause her to stretch her capabilities and thereby begin the process of learning how to avoid such crises in the future;
- He makes the initial and subsequent apportionments fully discussable between him and Trudy; and

- He makes his own and Trudy's performance subject to testing by one another as well by outsiders.

Were he to adopt this redefined stance, he would take a dramatically different approach to Trudy, a more learning-oriented approach that would cause her to take a more productive approach to followership. Rather than working independently and drifting apart, this redefinition would enable Larry and Trudy to work in true partnership in a way that would build and strengthen their relationship. Both could learn from one another. Trudy could learn administrative skills from Larry and Larry people-handling skills from Trudy.

Alternatively Trudy could take the initiative to follow a redefined approach to followership, which would have the effect of catalyzing a productive change in the leadership of Larry. In this situation, it would probably be considerably more difficult for Trudy to seize the initiative because she has never built her administrative and financial skills and would be too fearful to take the first step.

The Responsibility Ladder tool would be a great follow-on to the Redefinition of Leadership/Followership. Larry and Trudy could use this tool to apportion the responsibility with an eye to building Trudy's skills in managing her business to a point of independence.

As we've seen, the Responsibility Virus in daily life can be reined in using the same tools that have been developed for the world of large corporations. The Responsibility Ladder, the Choice Structuring Process, the Frame Experiment, and the Redefinition of Leadership/Followership can be used singly or in combination. The result will be better collaboration, healing of stressed or damaged relationships, and a faster pace of learning by all involved.

Recognizing and Fighting the Responsibility Virus

The Fear-of-Failure Irony

There is an Eastern European proverb that says that one cannot escape that of which one is most afraid. Ironically, it is the fear of failure that drives the behaviors that generate the Virus, which produces the failure that is so intensely feared in the first place. It's a vicious cycle: fear of failure generates more failure, which endlessly generates more fear and more failure.

Our current strategy for dealing with the fear of failure undermines our ability and willingness to engage in collaborative activities with others who would otherwise be valuable partners. It also drives us apart by spurring miscommunication, mistrust, and misunderstanding. While it is damaging our relationships with others, it is degrading our skill levels by causing our capabilities to make decisions and engage in meaningful collaborations to atrophy over time. Under the influence of the Responsibility Virus, we don't learn from failures. We simply repeat them.

The magnitude of the damage eludes easy measurement because the moment the Virus begins to cause failures, undermine collaboration, create misunderstanding, and produce atrophy, we lose touch with what might have been. It is impossible to measure what we've lost. We become comfortable with the self-imposed reality that we will have to forgo most collaborative opportunities. We accept relationships that are distant and uneasy rather than close and respectful because they feel as good as they can be, even when they are seriously flawed, and we become satisfied with capabilities that are nowhere near what they could have been.

What leads us to fear failure to such a degree that we will take these intensely counterproductive actions to avoid it? Our culturally reinforced, internal commitment to *win, not lose, maintain control, avoid embarrassment,* and *stay rational.*

We too often take extreme rather than balanced action in the face of our fear. We can become so paralyzed by the prospect of our own failure that we seek a level of responsibility well below our capabilities, thus driving others to take on responsibility in excess of their capabilities. Or, we can become so paralyzed by the prospect of the failure of others that we take on responsibility in excess of our own capabilities and cause those around us to lapse into apathy.

There are, however, tools at our disposal to fight that first and important step into the dynamic of the Virus. *The Choice Structuring Process* can help us work together in a fashion that minimizes the likelihood that we will feel motivated to seize or cede disproportionate responsibility as we work together, despite the lurking threat of failure. If we get into trouble while working together, we can recoup using

The Frame Experiment, a remedial tool for holding productive conversations under stressful conditions. By employing *The Responsibility Ladder,* a developmental tool, we can work on building our skills steadily while avoiding the detrimental effects of the Virus. Finally, we can avoid utilizing counterproductive definitions of roles by using *The Redefinition of Leadership and Followership.*

Taking Two to Tango

Virtually everyone with whom I discuss fighting the Responsibility Virus recognizes it in their lives but asks: "What can I *really* do by myself? So what if I change my behavior? I'm just one cog in a big wheel and if I change, everybody else will simply overwhelm me, especially those in positions of greater power than me. In fact, I'll get trampled. They'll try to 'win' and I'll end up losing consistently."

It feels a universally daunting and intimidating prospect to use the tools available to combat the Virus. But in fact, it isn't nearly so daunting in practice. That's because, thanks to the static conservation of responsibility, it truly takes two to tango. An over-responsible leader *needs* an under-responsible follower. And an under-responsible follower *needs* an over-responsible leader. Each provides the energy the other needs to sustain their part of the Virus.

The critical reality is that every one of us, in each specific situation, holds in our own hands the power to stop the Virus. All we have to do is refuse the opportunity presented to act over-responsibly or under-responsibly. Without our own cooperation, the would-be over-responsible leader or would-be under-responsible follower is incapable of launching the Responsibility Virus.

Vaclav Havel, the Czech playwright, dissident, and eventual president of the Czech Republic, understood the power of the individual and wrote persuasively about it in his inspirational essay "Power of the Powerless."[1] Written in 1978, long before the fall of the Berlin Wall and the crumbling of the Soviet empire, the essay took the form of a letter of encouragement to the striking Polish ship-workers at Gdansk. The outlawed Solidarity union had occupied the shipyards, but the authorities, rather than entering yards by force and arresting the strikers, a messy affair likely to be covered negatively by the international press, sought to starve and freeze the strikers into submission. Not a bad strategy in the cold Polish winter!

The workers no doubt felt largely powerless against the might of an arm of the powerful Soviet state, but Havel encouraged them to see their inherent power. He told of a shopkeeper in what was then the Soviet Union who was ordered to put a sign in his window reading "Workers of the world unite!" The shopkeeper knows the slogan is a hollow lie, but is inclined to put it in his window rather than face harsh retribution for civil disobedience. However, by putting the sign in his window, he sends a signal to all who pass that he is bowing to the will of the totalitarian state, and thereby strengthening it.

If instead the humble shopkeeper refuses to place the sign in his window and endures the punishment, he sends an incredibly powerful signal to the authorities and everyone who knows what he did, that the state is not omnipotent. This will cause the state to crumble, and crumble more quickly than anyone can imagine.

Havel's message to the strikers was to recognize that however powerless they felt, they had the power to crumble an empire. Prophetic words for 1978. The Polish strikers, with no ability to physically challenge Soviet power, unleashed a tidal wave of change that within a decade demolished the all-powerful Soviet state.

Havel's lessons apply equally to the more mundane world of the Responsibility Virus. The seemingly powerless individual is indeed full of power. Even though the Virus is everywhere and is reinforced by the norms of society and by our very instincts, we, as individuals, always have the ability to stop it. We can use the four tools to help us take baby steps in the right direction. We need no one's permission or concurrence. We simply need to act.

And we will be reinforced, not discouraged, in our course of action by those who feel the powerful, positive effects of our first tentative steps. By taking positive action, we have the effect of attracting our colleagues to balanced responsibility rather than pushing them to extremes of responsibility. They will feel better about us even if they have no idea why they do. If we frame our colleagues more positively, they will feel the beneficial effects in the nature of our questions and our demeanor toward them. If we use the Responsibility Ladder to take on just a bit more responsibility or dole out just a bit more, we will create a more positive world.

With each step, our skills in holding more productive responsibility conversations will grow, as will our ability to help others hold such conversations. Each time we confront failure without fear, we will learn to deal more productively with failure and advance our capabilities. As our experience and confidence grow, we accelerate the upward cycle of capabilities growth for ourselves, for those around us, and for our organizations in general.

Reflecting on Governing Values

By using the four tools, we can successfully fight the Responsibility Virus. However, the tools go no further than to counteract the negative consequences of the fundamental governing values: *win, don't lose; maintain control; avoid embarrassment;* and *stay rational.*

An even better strategy involves reflecting on and modifying the governing values that give rise to negative consequences in the first place. This is easier said than done, given that these governing values permeate every aspect of our society.[2] In fact, in certain ways, they are the glue that allows us to communicate and coordinate our actions.[3]

Each of the four tools assumes both the existence and the counterproductive power of the governing values. The Choice Structuring Process assumes that the members of the team in question are each imbued with the traditional governing values. It is designed to steer the team members clear of feeling that they are losing or that the situation may get out of control or get emotional or that they may suffer embarrassment. By doing so, the process minimizes counterproductive behavior and encourages productive behavior. The productive behavior provides encouragement to the group to be less obsessed by the fear of failure. In turn, that helps the group work productively toward choices. However, throughout the process, the governing values remain in place and lurk inches below the surface.

In a similar fashion, the Frame Experiment takes into account that the parties to the experiment are driven to their counterproductive frames by the same governing values. The Frame Experiment seeks to produce a better outcome by asking the participant(s) to temporarily put aside their counterproductive frame. Knowing how hard this will be, given the longstanding tenure of the governing values, it asks only for temporary adherence to the superior frame.

The Responsibility Ladder seeks to create small steps and a productive language system to overcome the natural tendency for leaders and followers to take on damaging extremes of responsibility, driven by the traditional governing values. And the Redefinition of Leadership and Followership seeks to overlay more productive mental models on the counterproductive values. In all cases, the tools compensate for but do not attack the mindset that dictates *win, don't lose; maintain control; avoid embarrassment;* and *stay rational.* With use of the four tools, frames and actions become more productive and results become more gratifying, yet lying beneath are the negative principles. The ultimate step is to replace each value with something more positive and productive.

Informed Choice Versus Win, Don't Lose

Rather than see *winning* as the highest value, we must replace it with the value of making the most *informed choice*, without regard to whose point of view it represents. The goal of making the most *informed choice* necessitates that we employ dialogue rather than depend on unilateralism. Unilateral choice fails to access and take into account the data, insights, experience, and interests of others, resulting in sub-optimal decisions. Only dialogue, made possible by curtailing our urge to win, will produce a more robust and *informed choice*.

Changing the governing value from *win, don't lose* to *informed choice* applies as well to choices about the division of responsibility. The *win, don't lose* value causes us to seize and cede responsibility unilaterally without consultation, bringing on the Responsibility Virus. The *informed choice* value drives us toward dialogue with the other involved parties about creating the optimal division of responsibilities. The sharing that results from such dialogue may not make us optimally comfortable and may not reflect our position going in, but we will draw greater benefit from a broader, deeper pool of data and insights than we would otherwise.

Internal Commitment Versus Maintain Control

The desire for *control* causes us to seize or cede extremes of responsibility to ensure that we either control everything or control virtually nothing. It also causes us to make choices unilaterally, without consultation with those who have valuable insight to add.

When we suppress our desire to *maintain control* and instead value generating *internal commitment*, we can engage in true dialogue and the exchange of ideas. The result of dialogue rather than unilateral choice is better distribution of responsibilities and better choices based on the logic and reasoning of both parties. This produces followers and leaders who are not merely acquiescent but genuinely and internally committed to the choices they have made together in an honest and open dialogue.

Open Testing Versus Avoid Embarrassment

When we take on extremes of responsibility unilaterally in order to avoid any conversation or discussion that would generate *embarrassment*, it not only makes for bad division of responsibility and bad choices but it fosters negligent oversight as well.

The surfacing, scrutinizing, and discussion of data on choice and performance that might produce learning and skill-building never happens, because it might also produce embarrassment for both the evaluator and evaluatee.

Applying *open testing* to all choices, whether made by others or by us, may subject us to more embarrassment, but it will also lead to better choices. And in the end, there is nothing more embarrassing than living with the consequences of a truly bad choice. If our choice turns out to have a bad result despite our best thinking, *open testing* will help us learn from the mistake and improve rather than repeat the same mistake.

Be Authentic Versus Stay Rational

In a truly misguided attempt to *stay rational* because we fear losing control of our emotions and creating embarrassment, we strive to bury our emotions deep inside and only argue from the rational elements of the issue at hand. However, no interaction or choice is 100 percent rational and devoid of emotional content. We only try to act as if it is that way—but the resulting lack of authenticity in our actions confuses those with whom we interact. They know emotions lurk under the surface of our rational arguments. They are simply left to guess exactly what those emotions are.

They can sense the negativity of these suppressed emotions—feelings of helplessness, betrayal, loneliness, disappointment, and more. So guessing begets misunderstanding, which begets mistrust. And as others suppress their emotions, we guess, misunderstand, and mistrust as well. The desperate attempt to suppress the emotional elements of our being cannot succeed, and, in fact, helps us fail.

When we instead give ourselves permission to *be authentic*, we enable ourselves to integrate our emotions with our logic. In doing so, we help others understand us better and encourage them to be authentic, which helps us understand them as well. And when we surface the emotional elements of an issue or decision or interaction, the emotional issues don't have to build up negative intensity deep inside us as we try to suppress the insuppressible.

Armed with the governing values of *informed choice*, *internal commitment*, *open testing*, and *authenticity*, we can forge relationships that are bilateral rather than unilateral. With these values, the extreme responses melt away and we are inclined to choose appropriate responsibility rather than over-responsibility or under-responsibility. And our choices are reflective rather than automatic. We reflect on choices before and after making them. With reflection and appropriate responsibility our capabilities will grow, not atrophy.

By living these values, we not only help ourselves, but we actually protect others from the Responsibility Virus. We reduce their inclination toward extremes of responsibility and bind them closer to the productive middle ground of responsibility. So we benefit all when we benefit ourselves with the new values.

Despite the compelling benefits, the thought of switching in one fell swoop from old values to new is unrealistic, even preposterous. The secret is to take baby steps in the right direction by gaining confidence in the four tools. Employing these tools will stimulate and reinforce choice-making and responsibility sharing under the alternative values.

Living on the Edge

In embracing a new set of governing values, we choose to live our lives on the forward edge of our capabilities. This new way will produce failure, but it will be failure of a distinctly better sort. The Responsibility Virus produces hopeless failures resulting from extreme mismatches of capabilities and responsibilities, which leads to cover-up rather than learning. Failures under the new set of governing values—I predict—will be failures at the margin of our capabilities—failure from setting responsibilities marginally too high. From this failure we will be able to learn immensely, because our analysis and reflection won't be circumscribed by fear.

With learning comes the enhancement of capabilities, not their decline. For each of us, the greatest level of self-actualization comes from building our capabilities steadily over time, but that requires submitting ourselves to a constant level of manageable stress. It also stems from coming to welcome, not resist, scrutiny of our performance by others. Stress guards against our under-responsibility and scrutiny discourages our potential over-responsibility.

Organizations populated with individuals living the new governing values, employing a redefined model of leadership, and holding more sophisticated conversations about responsibility will *seek* rather than *avoid* competitive forces to ensure that their capabilities will be stretched. Leadership of such organizations will be too busy competing to consider acting over-responsibly. Followers will ensure that they are stressing their capabilities and scrutinizing their leaders thoroughly. Organizations populated with such people will run circles around organizations held in the grip of the Responsibility Virus.

Each one of us has the capability to start a chain of events with huge power and leverage. As Havel demonstrated in Poland, we *do* hold the power in our hands.

Notes

Introduction

1. Janis, I., and R. Mann, *Decision Making*, New York: Free Press, 1977.

2. Festinger, L., *A Theory of Cognitive Dissonance*, Illinois: Row and Peterson, 1957.

3. Hegel, G. F. W. (1809), *Phenomenology of the Spirit*, (G. Miller, translation), Princeton: Princeton University Press, 1978.

4. Langer, E. J., *The Psychology of Control*, Beverly Hills, Calif.: Sage Publications, 1975.

5. Janis, I., *Groupthink: Psychological Studies of Policy Decisions and Fiascoes*, Boston: Houghton Mifflin, 1982.

6. Asch, S., "Opinions and Social Pressure," *Scientific American*, November 1955.

Chapter 1

1. Langer, *The Psychology of Control*, 1975.

2. Gilovich, T., *How We Know What Isn't So: Fallibility of Human Reasoning in Everyday Life*, New York: The Free Press, 1993.

271

Chapter 2

1. Numerous works by Chris Argyris can be accessed to understand his thinking on governing values, defensive routines, and patterns of reasoning. Four recent books provide excellent background:

Argyris, C., *Overcoming Organizational Defenses: Facilitating Organizational Learning*, Boston: Allyn & Bacon, 1990.

Argyris, C., *Knowledge for Action*, San Francisco: Jossey-Bass, 1993.

Argyris, C., *On Organizational Learning*, London: Blackwell, 1993.

Argyris, C., *Flawed Advice and the Management Trap: How Managers Can Know When They're Getting Good Advice and When They're Not*, New York: Oxford University Press, 1999.

The following five articles/book chapters provide earlier analyses of these issues:

Argyris, C., "Reasoning, Action Strategies and Defensive Routines: The Case of OD Practitioners," in *Research in Organizational Change and Development*, New York: JAI Press, 1987.

Argyris, C., "Making Knowledge More Relevant to Practice: Maps for Action," in E. E. Lawler III et al. (eds.), *Doing Research That Is Useful for Theory and Practice*, San Francisco: Jossey-Bass, 1985.

Argyris, C., "Dealing with Threat and Defensiveness," in J. Pennings and Associates (eds.), *Organizational Strategy and Change*, San Francisco: Jossey-Bass, 1985.

Argyris, C., "How Learning and Reasoning Processes Affect Organizational Change," in Paul S. Goodman and Associates (eds.), *Change in Organizations: New Perspectives on Theory, Research and Practice*, San Francisco: Jossey-Bass, 1982.

Argyris, C., "Do Personal Growth Laboratories Represent an Alternative Culture?," *The Journal of Applied Behavioral Science*, Volume 8, No. 1, 1972.

2. Greenwald, A., M. R. Leippe, A. R. Pratkannis, and M. H. Baumgardner, "Under What Conditions Does Theory Obstruct Research Progress?," *Psychological Review*, 93: 216–229 (1986).

Chapter 3

1. Aronson, E., *The Social Animal*, Englewood Cliffs, N.J.: Prentice Hall, 1993.

Chapter 4

1. Smith, A. (1793), *Inquiry into the Wealth of Nations*, New York: Penguin, 1982.
2. Von Hippel, E., *The Sources of Innovation*, New York: Oxford, 1988.
3. Baum, J. A. C., and F. Dobbin, "Economics Meets Sociology in Strategic Management," in *Advances in Strategic Management*, Stamford, Conn.: JAI Press, 2000.

Chapter 5

1. Klein, M., *New Directions in Psychoanalysis*, London: Tavistock, 1955.
2. Jaques, E., *The Changing Culture of a Factory*, London: Tavistock, 1951.
3. Nickerson, R., "How We Know—And Often Misjudge—What Others Know: Imputing One's Knowledge to Others," *Psychological Bulletin*, 125:737–759 (1999).
4. Fiske, S., and S. F. Taylor, *Social Cognition*, New York: McGraw-Hill, 1991, and Festinger, *A Theory of Cognitive Dissonance*, 1957.

Chapter 6

1. Locke, E. A., and G. P. Latham, *Goal Setting: A Motivational Technique That Works*, Englewood Cliffs, N.J.: Prentice Hall, 1984.
2. Csikszentmihalyi, M., *Flow: Studies in Enjoyment*, PHS Grant Report R01 HM 22883–02 (1974).

Chapter 7

1. Abelson, R., "Beliefs Are Like Possessions," *Journal for the Theory of Social Behavior*, Volume 16, No. 3 (1986).
2. Janis, *Groupthink: Psychological Studies of Policy Decisions and Fiascoes*, 1982.
3. Bowlby, J., *Attachment*, New York: Cambridge University Press, 1965.
4. Nickerson, *Psychological Bulletin*, 1999.
5. Argylis, *Overcoming Organizational Defenses: Facilitating Organizational Learning*, 1990.
6. The term "dueling ladders" was coined by a consulting colleague of mine, Diana Smith of Action Design.

Chapter 8

1. Newell, A., *Unified Theories of Cognition*, Cambridge, Mass.: Harvard University Press, 1991.
2. Lakoff, G., and M. Johnson, *Metaphors We Live By*, Chicago: University of Chicago Press, 1981.
3. Bazerman, M., *Managerial Judgments and Decision Making*, New York: John Wiley, 1995.
4. Lakoff, G., and M. Johnson, *Philosophy in the Flesh*, New York: Cambridge University Press, 1999.
5. Gilovich, *How We Know What Isn't So*, 1993.

6. Abelson, *Journal for the Theory of Social Behavior*, 1986.

7. Diana Smith introduced me to the concept of *The Frame Experiment* when we worked together on a consulting assignment. Thus far it exists only in unpublished work by Ms. Smith and her colleagues at Action Design.

Chapter 10

1. Cheng, P., and R. Nisbett, "Pragmatic Constraints on Causal Deduction," in R. Nisbett (ed.), *Rules for Reasoning*, Hillsdale, N.J.: Erlbaum, 1985.

Chapter 11

1. Seligman, M., *Learned Helplessness*, New York: Free Press, 1984.

Chapter 13

1. Abbott, A. D. G., *The System of the Professions*, Chicago: University of Chicago Press, 1988.

2. Moldoveanu, M. C., and N. Nohria, *Codes, Communication and Coordination*, manuscript, Harvard Business School and Rotman School of Management, University of Toronto, 2002.

Chapter 14

1. Jensen, M., and W. Meckling, "Theory of the Firm: Managerial Behavior, Agency Costs and Ownership Structure," *Journal of Financial Economics*, 1976, pp. 305–360.

2. Moldoveanu, M., and R. Martin, *Agency Theory and the Design of Efficient Governance Mechanisms*, Report to the Joint Committee on Corporate Governance, Rotman School of Management, 2001.

3. Moldoveanu and Martin, *Agency Theory and the Design of Efficient Governance Mechanisms*, 2001.

4. Ainslie, G., "Beyond Microeconomics," in J. Elster (ed.), *The Multiple Self*, New York: Cambridge University Press, 1985.

5. Moldoveanu and Martin, *Agency Theory and the Design of Efficient Governance Mechanisms*, 2001.

6. Moldoveanu and Martin, *Agency Theory and the Design of Efficient Governance Mechanisms*, 2001.

Conclusion

1. Havel, V., "Power of the Powerless," in *Open Letters*, Paul Wilson (ed.), New York: Knopf, 1991.

2. Fiske, A. P., "The Four Elementary Forms of Sociality: A Framework for a Unified Theory of Social Relations," *Psychological Review*, 99: 689–723 (1992).

3. Fukuyama, F., *The Great Disruption*, New York: Free Press, 1999.

Index